Bibliographic Instruction and Computer Database Searching

Library Orientation Series

(Most volumes are still in print;
the two out-of-print volumes are designated.)

Bibliographic Instruction and Computer Database Searching

Papers Presented at the
Fourteenth Library Instruction Conference
held at Eastern Michigan University
8 & 9 May 1986; and Numerous
Examples of Current
Instructional Materials Collected
in Late 1987

edited by
Teresa B. Mensching
Director, LOEX Clearinghouse

Keith J. Stanger
Coordinator of Access Services
University Library/Learning Resources
and Technologies
Eastern Michigan University

Published for Learning Resources and Technologies
Eastern Michigan University
by
Pierian Press
Ann Arbor, Michigan
1988

14541

ISBN 0-87650-251-6

Pierian Press
P.O. Box 1808
Ann Arbor, Michigan 48106

Table of Contents

Articles   1

Poster Session Abstracts   79

Discussion Group Handouts and Sample Materials

Appendixes   147

Bibliographies   153

Participants   169

PREFACE

The Fourteenth National LOEX Library Instruction Conference was held on 8 and 9 May 1986 at the Hoyt Conference Center of Eastern Michigan University. Sponsored by the LOEX Clearinghouse on Library Instruction, the 1986 meeting resumed a more formal format after the 1985 Second Biennial LOEX Workshop. By alternating a conference with a workshop each year, the LOEX office hopes to provide options and opportunities for more indepth practical experiences for interested participants.

The presentations, with the exception of the poster sessions, are printed in the order they were presented in an attempt to maintain the step-by-step format of this year's program, Bibliographic Instruction and Computer Database Searching.

This conference theme was chosen for obvious timely reasons: many requests on how to incorporate online searching services in existing programs of bibliographic instruction and library orientation have been received at the LOEX Clearinghouse, and the topic was a logical progression from last year's workshop on Instructing the Online Catalog User. In addition, sufficient significant progress in the field had been made for the LOEX Clearinghouse to identify at least eight BI librarians with expertise and experience to serve as potential speakers.

The meeting was designed to fill the needs of instruction librarians who were asking these questions: how will online training of library clients affect the direction of bibliographic instruction; how to coordinate the introduction of online bibliographic competencies; what are the problems and obstacles of identifying and training different users; what are the nuts and bolts of setting up a searching service; what methods and modes are workable; which specific training programs have been properly evaluated; how is the service financed?

The main consideration of participants was how computer searching is being integrated into library instruction, and whether the service would be an add-on, mentioned at the end of a lecture, or the actual mechanism through which the principles of search strategy and the evaluation of library tools are to be taught.[1] Does the librarian teach the patron how to do his or her own search, or should the librarian provide the information as the intermediary? If the librarian is usually obliged to do the actual searching and, therefore, the quality of the search product doesn't depend on the user's knowledge or skill, what is gained from the added expense, time, and effort of educating that user?[2] By the end of the conference, consensus seemed to point to the opinion that explaining the online search process will help the library user to better understand the concepts of information seeking and its meaning for scholarship. Speakers also stressed the importance of having the library professional take the initiative for establishing the computer-searching services and training programs on campus.

These proceedings also include reprints of library-produced handouts that relate to instructing the database user, bibliographies on the topic, poster session abstracts, and a list of conference attendees.

As always, the LOEX Conference staff is grateful to all those who assisted in making the meeting a success--to the competent speakers, to Hannelore Rader for contributing her annual bibliography, to Vicky Young who helps the LOEX staff at each annual meeting, to Oak Woods Media for providing financial support in helping to sponsor our parties, to the helpful Hoyt Conference Center staff, and especially to each enthusiastic participant who contributed to the cohesive and cooperative atmosphere that seems to fortuitously pervade each LOEX meeting.

Mensching is Director of LOEX Clearinghouse, and **Stanger** is Coordinator of Access Services, at Eastern Michigan University, Ypsilanti, MI.

NOTES

1. Carol Tobin, "Online Computer Bibliographic Searching as an Instructional Tool, *Reference Services Review* 12 (Winter 1984): 72.

2. Thelma Freides, "Current Trends in Academic Libraries," *Library Trends* 31 (Winter 1983): 465.

Taking a Leadership Role in

End-User Instruction

Joan K. Lippincott

INTRODUCTION

It is time for professional librarians of all types to transfer their bibliographic organization and retrieval skills to the contemporary information environment. In so doing, we must also prepare our users for the realities and challenges of coping with information today. As librarians involved in the educational mission of colleges and universities, we need a vision of the kinds of skills students and faculty must acquire to aid them in their studies and future careers. It is incumbent upon librarians in academe to take a leadership role in planning and conducting education in information organization and retrieval for their constituencies.

Developing and offering an end-user instruction program is an important means for librarians to prepare students and faculty to handle information today and into the future. It is one component of an information literacy program which teaches individuals about the variety of sources of information, how information is used in the disciplines, how information is retrieved, how researchers keep up-to-date, how information is evaluated, and how information can best be organized for personal use or dissemination.

End-user instruction generally refers to the process of teaching individuals to search online bibliographic databases. Those who will use the end product of the search, usually a bibliography, perform the search themselves rather than having an intermediary run the search. End-user instruction as a term is generally not applied to teaching individuals to use an online library catalog. However, the principles, concepts, and methods for online

Lippincott is Head of Public Services Mann Library, Cornell University Ithaca, NY.

Joan K. Lippincott 1

catalog instruction are generally the same as for instruction in searching such databases as PsycINFO, BIOSIS, and ERIC.

While end-user searching programs have been attempted for a number of years, generally in special libraries, the impetus to launch such programs in the academic environment came in the early 1980s with the introduction of user-friendly, menu-driven, and simplified searching systems. Major database vendors such as Dialog, BRS, and Information Access saw the opportunity to market databases directly to consumers using home personal computers. Dialog and BRS did not seek to reach the academic audience through their long-time supporters the librarians; rather they approached faculty, students, businessmen, doctors, and scientists through direct mail campaigns and ads in personal computing magazines. Their promotional literature never mentioned the words library or librarian or indicated a relationship between their services and printed indexes and abstracts or collections of materials for retrieval of references identified through searching.

Many librarians seemed content with their non-involvement in the new arena of end-user searching. Individual faculty on their campuses purchased passwords and began searching; some faculty even began instruction programs for their students. The idea of adding yet another service to an already over-burdened reference department seemed too difficult to contemplate and the librarians accepted their passive role without comment.

In other libraries, the online searching coordinator became interested in the concept of end-user searching and began to advise faculty and students on how to use these services. In fewer cases, the library instruction coordinator saw the potential of these new services and began to incorporate end-user searching into the overall instruction program.

In general, however, the profession's reaction to end-user searching has been lukewarm. Even librarians who are interested in principle often refrain from attempting implementation of programs due to several factors. Chief among these is cost: concern that users, particularly undergraduate students, would not be interested in paying for searches. Also, many librarians doubt the general utility and wisdom of teaching students online searching when printed tools could adequately fulfill their needs. Librarians also are concerned that online searching is much too complex to be taught to the average student audience.

A *laissez-faire* attitude towards end-user searching could have serious consequences for the role of academic librarians in the institutions they serve. Others less qualified will take on the role of bibliographic searching expert, we will sacrifice

our credibility, and we will abdicate our responsibility for our own field of expertise.

Of course, a fundamental question is whether or not end-users need to be taught to search online bibliographic databases. The vendors certainly did not intend their user-friendly systems to need instruction. A distinction needs to be made, however, between the ease of using the system protocol and the complexities of developing and executing a workable search strategy. The latter skills definitely require some forms of instruction.

Librarians are particularly well-suited to teach end-user searching. We have the requisite bibliographic skills, an understanding of the composition and limitations of databases, an overview of the range of information sources, and an understanding of such fundamental concepts as controlled vocabulary, free text searching, access points, search strategy, and Boolean operators.

Some librarians, however, need to change their own assumptions and attitudes in order to develop a true commitment to end-user instruction in the academic environment. First, there is the assumption that students must understand print tools before they are exposed to online searching. Is there truly a clear rationale for stating that learning about access points, subject terminology, search strategy, and interpretation of bibliographic records is better or more fundamental in print tools than in online databases? Second, a limiting assumption is that students' needs are not complex enough to benefit from online database searching. The reality is that students prefer conducting their own online searches to any other type of information retrieval. Also, students will generally have more complex needs as they advance in the educational institution and as they go into professional careers. Preparing students for the long-term while having them gain skills through relatively straightforward searches seems to be a logical teaching method. Third, there is concern that online searching skills are too complex to teach to students. The assumption underlying this point of view is that our goal is to teach students search skills that are commensurate with those of librarians. This is not necessary and in most cases not desirable. Students do need to understand the limitations of their search skills, however.

If librarians do accept the challenge and take a leadership role in end-user searching instruction, what are the benefits to them? Increased visibility on campus is almost assured. Many faculty and administrators are struggling to understand microcomputer applications and will welcome the library's willingness to share its expertise in this new area. It is likely that faculty will seek librarians out for an introduction to online searching and might request private search tutorials. The collegiality of such relationships enhances the image of librarians and sets the stage for cooperation in other library matters. The computer services division on campus may also welcome an attempt by the library to develop an end-user instruction program. They can remain more concerned with computational and administrative needs. A joint instruction effort might be mounted whereby computer services staff teach an introduction to microcomputers (hardware, software, and communications) and the library follows with a session on searching online databases. The lasting value of cooperative efforts with computer services should not be underestimated. A quite different reward of developing an end-user instruction program is the enthusiastic response of faculty and students. Many are truly excited as they print out the results of their first search. Their keen interest and enthusiasm are a terrific morale boost for librarians. Developing a program that leads to this happy result requires thought and planning. First, goals and objectives need to be considered.

GOALS AND OBJECTIVES

Developing goals and objectives for an end-user instruction program is instrumental in defining what the librarian hopes the students will accomplish and in laying the ground-work for the instructional plan. Goals can vary widely depending on the types of users, the sophistication they bring to the instructional environment, the level of searching skill to be attained, and the ultimate use of the searching skills. Some sample goals statements are:

- Students will become familiar with the availability, advantages, and disadvantages of conducting their own bibliographic database searches and they will be able to perform the necessary procedures to run basic searches in a given online system.
- Students will understand the skills and concepts necessary for searching bibliographic databases and will be able to transfer these skills and concepts to other online systems. Students will be motivated to use online systems and will approach them with confidence.

The first goal emphasizes development of an understanding of what online searching is all about and attainment of a basic skill level. The following goal also emphasizes understanding, but broadens the focus to include transfer of knowledge and skills; it also includes an affective component. Transferability of skills is very important in end-user instruction. Users may have access to numerous information systems in their academic and professional careers. They should be able to make informed judgments about the usefulness of different systems and be able to understand them according to generic criteria such as access points, power of the search software, and vocabulary structure.

Often the affective components of end-user instruction programs are not clearly stated as goals. The confidence with which students use online information systems is of more academic significance than general computer literacy skills.

A goal statement for a faculty program could be one of the above or could have different emphases. Two such goal statements are:

- Faculty will understand the skills and concepts necessary for searching bibliographic databases. They will be able independently to use online database systems to perform routine verification, current awareness, and quick information searches. They will be motivated to use online systems in their daily work.

or

- Faculty will be able and motivated to use online database systems to fulfill all of their bibliographic information needs, from simple to comprehensive. They will have a thorough knowledge of databases in their field and will use sophisticated searching techniques.

Objectives should be developed from goal statements. Whether they are written in strict behavioral format is a debatable issue, but they will always serve as an excellent guideline for deciding what to include in an instructional session. Several of the goals statements mentioned earlier included "understanding the skills and concepts necessary for searching bibliographic databases." Specifically, those skills and concepts should include understanding what a bibliographic database is, advantages and disadvantages of online searching, what controlled vocabulary and free-text mean, how to choose terms for a search, how to group a topic into concepts or sets, how to link sets with Boolean operators, how to input and print out a search, and how and when to look for supplemental information. Sample objectives are:

- Students can define a bibliographic database and give an example of a database.
- Students can list advantages and disadvantages of computer searching as compared to a manual search and recognize conditions when a computer search is likely to be more effective than a manual search.

- Given an appropriate thesaurus, students can choose relevant terms for their topic and can add free text words as needed.
- Students can construct a logical search strategy for their topic by identifying subject concepts and using Boolean operators to link terms and manipulate sets.
- Students can use an online menu to independently input their search strategy on a terminal or microcomputer and execute the steps needed to print out citations.
- Students can recognize situations in which their online search needs to be supplemented by further computer searching and/or expertise.

In programs for students, generally the library will control the choice of vendor system and the hardware and software used. However, faculty may wish to open their own searching accounts and configure their own microcomputers for searching. Suitable objectives to add in this situation would be:

- Faculty can analyze their searching needs and can make judgments on which vendor's system would serve them best.
- Faculty can list the hardware and software needed for online searching.

In addition, faculty may have needs for particular types of searches which require specialized searching skills. They may also want to understand how online searching can be used to develop a personal reference file. Objectives for these situations would be:

- Faculty can conduct author and citation searches in databases appropriate to their field.
- Faculty can describe how online searching can interface with a bibliographic file management package.

Clearly thinking out the goals and objectives of the program is imperative to its success. As the program develops, there will be a need for some kind of evaluation. The evaluation may attempt to measure the achievement of the goals and objectives, may be used as a tool to increase administrative support, or may measure the satisfaction of the students. Ultimately it is important to measure the long-range impact of end-user searching programs. Longitudinal studies should survey how frequently individuals search, how their attitudes towards use of online information systems change, and their view of the usefulness of the library's instruction program. Evaluation can provide the means for modifying the program or reaffirming its importance. In addition, many other concerns need to be examined.

PLANNING CONSIDERATIONS

Once there is a commitment to begin an end-user searching program under the auspices of the library, what kinds of things need to be addressed in the planning process? First, the political climate of the library and of the institution needs to be examined. Within the library is there administrative support for the program? The program will require funds and a shift in staff assignments. Since the program will affect a number of staff not involved with the program, will they lend their support? Within the institution, are there departments or individual faculty who can serve as the opinion leaders who will help promote the program? Any instruction program needs to be built on a strong foundation in order to grow and thrive. Which group or groups to target for a pilot program is an important decision. Ideally, this group should be from a politically influential department, have particularly pressing needs for access to online databases, and be able to contribute financially to the program. Often the best publicity the library gets is from satisfied users. If the intent is to expand the program, begin with a group that will help advertise it.

The type of end-user searching program established may well be a reflection of the overall instruction program of the library. Formats include:

- reference service (no formal instruction)
- course-related
- workshop
- course (usually for credit)
- self-paced

The end-user searching program may be considered an extension of reference service, with assistance provided individually only as needed. A course-related approach will probably be chosen by those who believe that instruction is most effective when integrally related to students' course assignments. Independent workshops may be chosen as the format for some groups, particularly faculty, for whom this would be logical. Highly motivated graduate students, especially in departments without core courses, may also be good candidates for independent workshops. Some libraries may choose a course format, especially when their goal is to prepare students or faculty to achieve a high level of searching skill. The self-paced instructional format can include workbooks, CAI, and microcomputer tutorials. Preparation of materials for such programs is initially very time-consuming but may result in later savings in staff time.

Aside from the formal instruction component, decisions need to be made about ongoing assistance for end-user searchers. Will librarians consult on search strategy formulation? How and when will that activity be staffed? Will users have coaching assistance during their searches? Will librarians consult with faculty interested in setting up their own equipment and their own accounts?

Planning the format of the end-user searching program will also bring to the fore questions about staffing. Decisions will need to be made about how many staff need to be involved, what level of staff (librarian, support staff, students), what functions they will carry out, and how they will be scheduled.

Administrative considerations, particularly the budget, are critical in the planning process. End-user instruction programs reported in the literature often seem to have a life of only a semester or a year. How students will continue to search online databases after they have acquired the skills is often not made clear. The budget should include both start-up costs and estimates of the financial resources needed to maintain and expand the program. Specific items in the budget include equipment needs, any extra staff, teaching materials, and funds for staff training on the system(s) chosen. In large programs, facilities are also a major concern. Not only are extra terminals or microcomputers needed, but a separate room with its own telephone lines, a microcomputer projector, software, manuals, and thesauri need to be considered.

A decision on which vendors' system(s) to be offered must be carefully thought out. Will a smorgasbord of systems be available or will users be limited to one? Factors to be considered when choosing a system include cost, hours of availability, databases available, hardware and software needed, and ease of use. Librarians should survey the market and weight the needs of their audience against the strengths and weaknesses of the available systems. A decision based on past familiarity with a vendor's system or the persuasiveness of a salesman may end up short-changing users.

The sources of funding for the end-user searching program and the charging structure are inextricably linked. Generally the library underwrites the start-up and overhead costs of the program, either through the regular budget or by means of a special allocation from the regular budget or by means of a special allocation from the university or parent institution. For the ongoing costs, primarily the vendor charges for the actual searching time, four options are available. First, the library may absorb the full cost of online end-user searching. A number of libraries already fully subsidize intermediary searching and could add the end-user component to their program. Often these libraries place some type of limitations on the users. Second, libraries can charge users all direct costs of the search, as many already do with their intermediary searches. Third, librarians can attempt to secure funding from departments, special programs, or administrators to subsidize searching charges. In recent years, funding for computer literacy programs for both faculty and students has been made available on many campuses. The library can make a case that an end-user instruction program is an excellent way to introduce students and faculty to a highly relevant and useful microcomputer application. Fourth, a combination of the funding sources can be used. For example, a department might subsidize half of the charges and the students or the library could pay the remainder.

Since many librarians are seriously concerned that an end-user searching program will not be successful if they need to charge their users, particularly undergraduates, a concerted effort to secure alternate sources of funding should be made during the planning process. This issue may resolve itself in the future due to new developments in technology.

FUTURE DIRECTIONS

Even two or three years ago, few college or university libraries would have imagined owning a number of large standard bibliographic databases. However, in a very short period of time, that has become possible. Local ownership of bibliographic databases will probably be the single most important factor in ensuring the inevitability of end-user searching. Large databases will be stored locally on mainframes, on microcomputers equipped with hard disks, and on compact disks.

What are the implications for academic libraries? Perhaps most importantly, local ownership should mean the end of searching charges. In the past, many institutions were opposed to using library funds for access to external databases; opposition against using acquisitions funds was most vociferous. However, now libraries are being given a choice to purchase databases, and as charging for access to locally owned materials is contrary to most libraries' philosophy, users will generally have free access. The rationale for maintaining subscriptions to print tools when the library owns the material in machine-readable format will be called into question.

Librarians will initially need to teach several search protocols to users: one for the online catalog, one for a particular vendor's CD-ROM system, one for an online system. The multiplicity of techniques may be confusing to users and difficult to master. The more that instruction emphasizes generic skills, the more hope there will be for transferability of knowledge. In the future, ideally users will have access to many databases through one gateway, perhaps the online catalog, and will need to understand only one system's protocol. On the other hand, as users gain basic information retrieval and computer literacy skills and come to the academic environment better prepared in those areas, we may be able to increase the sophistication of our instruction.

The field of library and information science is changing rapidly and has the potential for great impact on our users. If librarians take a leadership role in end-user searching instruction, they will help their audience cope with the information revolution in an informed and sophisticated way.

TARGETING AUDIENCES FOR AN END-USER SEARCHING PROGRAM

1. What group(s) do/would you target at your home institution? Why? (Factors to consider include level of the group, need for use of bibliographic references, limitations of available printed sources, and "political" factors.)

2. What system(s) do/would you teach each group? Why? (Factors to consider include availability of needed databases, hours of system availability, average number of references needed, complexity of topics, and cost.)

3. What form does/would your instruction take? Why? (Choices would include courses, course-related instruction, workshops, one-to-one tutoring, CAI, and use of printed materials.)

4. How do/would you fund the service? (Choices include direct payment by users, department or program subsidization, library subsidization, or a combination of factors.)

End-User Search Services in Academic Libraries:

Results from a National Study

Ilene F. Rockman

The status of end-user bibliographic instruction programs at this particular point in time is rather fluid and in a state of transition. Many libraries are on the precipice of embarking upon major policy decisions concerning the amount of autonomy end-users will enjoy in utilizing automated literature retrieval services. Almost ten years ago, it was predicted that end-users would "take over the terminal" and in several libraries that day is here.[1]

Changes in the automation industry have contributed to changes in library end-user policies. These changes have included: 1) an accelerated increase in the number of microcomputers with modems being used in the laboratory, office, and home environment; 2) new types of front-end and gateway software intended to make searching easier and more convenient for the infrequent, novice user; 3) a reduction in the amount of search costs for databases used during non-peak times rather than during what is considered to be prime hours; 4) menu-driven systems now available during the daytime; 5) end-user searching of internal and external databases with re-use of information from secondary sources downloaded for the creation of personal information systems; and 6) flexible billing options and charging frameworks, including the introduction of special educator rates for classroom-based instruction, the elimination of minimum usage fees, the allowance of fees assessed for only those searches that actually retrieve data, and capabilities for the acceptance of users' personal credit card numbers rather than the exclusive reliance upon charges to the library.

The role of the librarian has also undergone a change from search intermediary to pre-search

Rockman is End-User Services Coordinator, California Polytechnic State University Library San Luis Obispo, CA.

counselor, coach, or advisor. Although the optimal type of human instruction necessary to support a successful end-user search service is still unclear, these services become mainstays of academic libraries, rather than mere novelties.

Libraries are faced with the decision to offer stand-alone, self-service programs, course-integrated end-user instruction, separate librarian-taught courses, or a combination of these instructional strategies.

For these reasons, and because of the emergence of new delivery methods of database information in the form of laser and optical-based disk systems, a national study of end-user search services in selected four-year college and university libraries was undertaken in the fall of 1985.

OBJECTIVES OF THE STUDY

The objectives of the investigation were to gather information on ten separate variables. These are:

1. The types and formats of end-user systems currently offered in academic libraries.
2. The modes of instruction and types of instructional materials employed.
3. The clientele served and user characteristics.
4. The disciplines most heavily searched.
5. Evaluation methods and techniques.
6. Administration models and funding sources.
7. Hours of availability.
8. Types and levels of staffing.
9. Perceived advantages of offering an end-user service.
10. Problems and obstacles to overcome.

Although the library literature is replete with a multitude of articles and studies chronicling end-user search services, most reports fall into the category of either case studies, descriptions of particular library experiences, or comparative analyses of various software packages or services. Therefore, my inquiry sought to achieve a broader based view of the status of academic end-user services by identifying a multiplicity of factors important to consider in establishing and maintaining a service, and from the extent and magnitude of the results, to suggest which factors may be more salient to consider than others.

METHODOLOGY

The methodology selected for the study was that of survey research, and more specifically, mail survey research. Data was collected from a national sample of seventy academic librarians known to be engaged in end-user searching. No attempt was made to select a random sample of librarians. Instead, persons were contacted from directory listings generated by the Computer Concerns Committee of the ACRL Bibliographic Instruction Section, the Direct Patron Access to Computer-Based Reference Systems Committee of the RASD Machine-Assisted Reference Section, the Library Instruction Round Table of the American Library Association, and the California Clearinghouse on Library Instruction of the California Library Association. No attempt was made to provide a balance by type of library, geographic location, size of library, or type of end-user program.

A direct-mail, self-administered original forty-item instrument served as the data gathering tool. The actual mailing of the instrument occurred on 7 October 1985. A cover letter was included with each questionnaire to assure the respondents that their answers would be treated with anonymity and confidentiality. The enclosure of a self-addressed, stamped envelope encouraged the prompt return of the instrument. A follow-up postcard was sent two and a half weeks after the initial mailing to ask for the respondents' cooperation in either returning the questionnaire as soon as possible, or requesting a replacement copy if the original instrument was misplaced. Of the seventy individuals selected for the study, forty-eight (or 69 percent) responded, and of these, thirty were deemed valid for use. Those responses declared invalid were excluded from consideration due to the refusal of the respondents to answer all or a majority of the questions, or because the instrument was completed by an individual other than the one selected for the study.

Data were analyzed using non-parametric techniques. Because of multiple responses or lack of responses in some instances, no attempt was made to have the responses total the number of cases. Rather, the objective was to simply use frequency distributions to present a snapshot view of the status of end-user search services at a particular point in time.

QUESTIONNAIRE

The questionnaire was divided into five sections:

1. Type of system or system offered, which listed forty-seven different types representative of front ends, gateways, menu-driven, command-driven, optical-based, and computer-based systems tied to telecommunication networks.

2. Method of instruction. I was keenly interested to learn how users were *initially* instructed (if at all), what instructional materials were made available to help them (my definition of an end-

user being a novice, part-time user), and if a separate classroom-based hands-on course for students was offered. I purposely did not query respondents about seminars, workshops, or course-integrated instructional programs since much of this information is already documented in the library literature.

3.   The third category focused on users. I was interested to learn what user restrictions might be placed upon the service, if university and non-university affiliated users enjoyed equal access, who (in reality) actually used the system, the percentage of overall and repeat users, and the subjects most heavily searched.

4.   The next category was administration. I wanted to learn how the day-to-day operations of the service was managed, if the service was a temporary or a permanent feature of the library's instructional program, how the service was funded, how it was staffed, the level of staffing support, the hours of availability, the type of equipment, and the number and location of terminals.

5.   A section titled "Your Experiences" was added to solicit responses concerning the advantages and disadvantages of having the service, and to generate reactions about those factors thought to be of primary importance to the operation of a successful search service.

6.   The last section of the questionnaire gathered demographic data concerning the size of institution, the highest degree awarded, and number of searcher-librarians presently on the staff.

The questionnaire concluded with a blank section asking for additional comments or providing the opportunity for respondents to elaborate upon a previous answer. Many librarians were pleased to ventilate their frustrations or to enthusiastically share their success stories.

RESULTS

Of the forty-seven end-user systems listed on the questionnaire, only one-third were actually available to users, with much variation among libraries as to a system standard and no homogeneous response pattern. The most popular system offered among those surveyed was BRS/After Dark. Because of relative accounting ease, BRS/After Dark and Search Helper were offered more frequently than other services, despite annotated comments in the margins of the questionnaire concerning software problems and other inconveni-

ences.   Several libraries indicated plans to drop Search Helper for Wilsearch. Of those libraries that indicated using InfoTrac, many used the CD-ROM system because of a temporary free loan arrangement with the Information Access Company. These libraries could not state with certainty whether their institutions would continue the service, or whether their libraries would commit funds to purchasing the system once the trial loan period had expired, even though the annual subscription cost was a fixed fee and their students enjoyed using a free optical disk system accessed by a microcomputer. Several libraries had plans to add subscriptions to Easynet, the dial-up gateway service that offers a special library or institutional rate. Most libraries preferred having menu-driven systems for their users, rather than relying upon command or native mode searching systems.

In terms of instruction, more than half of the librarians completing the questionnaire reported that initial instruction to their users occurred on demand by a librarian, rather than as part of a course lecture, seminar, or tour. Worksheets were viewed as the preferred form of instructional material. Surprisingly, only two libraries amongst those surveyed offered a formal, credit-bearing course. Each class was offered only once; one as a summer seminar for teachers. A different respondent mentioned that a non-credit weekend seminar for faculty was taught by librarians, but that there were no plans to modify the information presented as a credit course for students. Therefore, it was somewhat disappointing that I did not locate new information about end-user credit courses, but understandable considering how labor-intensive such courses are.

Evaluation techniques reported in the library literature commonly include self-designed, written appraisal instruments that measure patron satisfaction. This form of evaluation can sometimes result in deceptive and inflated information being reported, and may not be the most valid and reliable method to gauge results. Often patron satisfaction is presumed to be equated with patron understanding, but approval of the search results does not necessarily indicate that skills have been learned to successfully and systematically find needed information. Therefore, I was curious to discover if unobtrusive or other evaluation techniques were incorporated into the evaluation process.

The most popular evaluation method was that of the solicited user questionnaire. Although the contents of these instruments were not disclosed by the respondents, typically they often include questions focusing upon user satisfaction, ease and versatility of software, cost effectiveness, depth of coverage, and speed with which the information is accessed. Those interested in examining examples of evaluation tools should consult the excellent

ARL Spec Kit on the topic.[2]

No library surveyed restricted the end-user system to only librarians for such uses as ready reference or inexpensive mediated searches. Instead, all libraries provided access to on-campus and non-university affiliated members, although the greatest usage did occur among first-timers who were predominately undergraduates searching for information related to the disciplines of business and finance, social science, current news topics, or education and psychology topics. This response may reflect the liberal arts focus of most libraries answering the questionnaire. The percentage of repeat users was less than half, which may have been indicative of the newness of the service in many libraries.

Administratively, most libraries delegated the day-to-day operation and responsibility of the service to the coordinator of online searching, but a large number of libraries reported dividing this responsibility between others including a database services committee, evening and weekend librarians, or branch librarians (if the service was in a decentralized institution).

More than half of the librarians surveyed offered end-user systems as a permanent feature of total library service. Perhaps because of the newness of the technology at the time of the survey, the rapidity with which it changes, and the uncertainty of costs associated with mounting and maintaining a service, the others still considered their offerings as pilot projects.

These services were funded in a variety of ways. The majority of the libraries did not charge their users, but instead, covered the costs from the general library budget. Others did charge user fees, or covered the costs from university grants, academic departmental allocations, or the book budget. Half of the libraries did not charge users, but those that did, levied charges by the minute or block of time, by the number of searches conducted, or on a cost recovery basis.

Search services appeared to be available at all times, but most frequently during the evening hours or on the weekends. These times parallel availability of BRS/After Dark, the system reported to have the largest usage among the respondents surveyed. The majority of libraries indicated that they staffed the end-user service with librarians, rather than with non-professionals, and that the average number of searcher-librarians amongst the libraries survey was nine.

The majority of libraries have located the service near the main reference desk, but many have chosen to place it away from the reference desk, although within the confines of the reference department. Microcomputer terminals outnumber dumb terminals by a two-to-one margin, with most libraries owning their own equipment and making available one or two terminals for users.

When asked to comment upon the advantages of having an end-user system, librarians indicated five predominant reasons:

- Increased user satisfaction with the library
- Enhanced campus image for the library
- Access to current information
- Low cost
- Ease of use.

Surprisingly, they volunteered these responses:

- Improved access to periodical indexes
- Increased user awareness of online services
- People come to the reference desk for help, and then we can teach them about print sources (a new twist on an old theme)
- There are few advantages.

Without a doubt, the librarians surveyed felt that there were more disadvantages than advantages, but these feelings may have been reflective of the types of systems used. In rank order, they reported disadvantages as:

- Increased staff workload
- Ill-prepared users
- Machine malfunctions
- Restrictive search results
- Less use than expected
- Restrictive hours
- Downtime
- Increased ILL activity.

They volunteered these responses:

- High cost
- Lack of training materials
- Poorly designed software
- Difficult commands
- Users think that the library has all the periodicals retrieved from the system.

When asked to consider the most important variables contributing to the success of an end-user search system, the librarians surveyed indicated in rank order the following:

- User training
- Staff training
- Administrative support
- Quality of software
- Space
- Staff acceptance
- Quality of hardware
- Publicity.

They volunteered:

- Quality of documentation
- Search lab facilities
- Low cost
- Presearch counseling.

Half of the libraries in the study represented doctoral-level institutions, with a third characteristic of post-baccalaureate universities. Only one respondent indicated that the library's primary mission was to support undergraduate education.

SUMMARY

The willingness of librarians to share information with this investigator was greatly appreciated. The magnitude of the end-user programs available six months ago was surprising, and encouraging to those libraries still deciding upon the most appropriate path to take for their own users. Results showed that end-user services were not always enthusiastically embraced by staff members, and included a variety of different types of services. Libraries seem to be groping with issues such as user education, funding, cost effectiveness, and staffing configurations, yet seem to be supplementing systems or substituting one system for another, rather than abandoning the practice of offering users the opportunity to conduct their own searches.

In terms of initial instructional offerings, stand-alone programs seem to be the most popular, with the role of the librarian running the gamut from one-on-one instructor to presearch counselor. Although many systems are menu-driven and meant to be self-service and relatively easy for the novice user to operate, librarians have sought to supplement vendor-provided documentation with a variety of instructional materials.

Although I did not specifically ask librarians why their libraries decided to offer end-user search services, through informal discussions across the country I have learned that rarely has the decision been based on an overload of mediated searches. Rather, librarians felt that students deserve to be made aware of, and exposed to, the latest forms of information technology, in concert with campus computer literacy efforts, and online catalog instruction. There is an expressed or perceived need to offer the service, and users appear to embrace the systems due to their curiosity and fascination with new technologies.

However, librarians have reported dissatisfaction with end-users who are not adequately prepared to analyze, clarify, refine, and translate an intellectual inquiry into a successful online retrieval topic, who lack the necessary skills to prepare and design search strategies likely to achieve relevant results, who may not understand the relationship between search output and library holdings, and often do not understand how to interpret, evaluate, and read citations. These broad comments support earlier studies that have identified user problems in choosing a database, selecting and entering search terms, understanding Boolean logic, and refining or modifying search topics to make the results more precise.[3] The complexities of the psychological and cognitive processes involved in developing good search skills by neophytes are still being underestimated.[4]

What does the future hold? More course-integrated and classroom-based instruction? Librarian presearch counseling, consultation, and professional guidance as the accepted convention? From the results of this investigation, it appears that any effort to establish and sustain an end-user search service may be predicated upon high quality software and hardware, plus a collaborative effort between administration and staff to commit time, space, personnel, and resources. The policy decision of whether or not to offer the service, however, is an individual matter, and libraries will have to wrestle with the question of deciding if they have an obligation to provide end-user search facilities as patrons bring to the library a new behavior pattern for seeking information.

The combination of end-user search systems aggressively marketed in new forms by database vendors; changes in software designs as exemplified by front-end packages, laser-based CD-ROM units, gateway interfaces or expert systems meant to simplify and standardize retrieval commands; and an increasing number of full-text files will all continue to challenge librarians in their quest to choose the most appropriate search service configuration for their specific client groups. Technology will continue to function as a change agent, and the role of the librarian may continue to be re-defined as advisor, consultant, counselor, educator, intermediary, policy-maker, soothsayer, or trouble-shooter, but will apparently not be replaced. Information will continue to proliferate, end-users will continue to seek it, and the innovative library will be the one that best addresses the needs of its users.

SURVEY RESULTS

Type of System(s)

1. End-User systems offered

BRS/After Dark	15
Search Helper	6
InfoTrac	6
BRS/BRKTHRU	4
Wilsearch	4
Knowledge Index	3
Easynet	2
Dow Jones News/Retrieval	1
ERIC MICROSearch	1
Paperchase	1

Instruction

2a. End-Users are *initially* instructed by a librarian

On demand	20
Course-integrated lecture	12
Seminar or workshop	10
Orientation or tour	7
Online demonstration	1

2b. Instructional materials *initially* used are

Worksheets	14
Operating manuals	11
Brochures	8
Annotated sample searches	6
Signs	5
Flip charts	2
Audio-visual presentations	2
Computer-assisted tutorials	2

Separate Course

3. Is a classroom-based, hands-on course for students offered?

Yes	2
No	25

Evaluation

4. Evaluation techniques used

Solicited user questionnaire	11
Observations by library staff	9
Discussions with users	2
Unsolicited user questionnaires	1
No formal evaluation	1

Users

5. The end-user system is available to

Students	27
Faculty members	26
Staff members	21
Non-university community	8

6. The end-user system is used by

Students	27
Faculty members	21
Librarians	19
Staff members	14
Non-university community	8

7. The largest percentage of users are

Undergraduates	19
Graduate students	7
Librarians	2

8. The percentage of repeat users is

Less than 25 percent	8
26 percent to 50 percent	7
51 percent to 75 percent	0
76 percent to 100 percent	1

9. Subjects most heavily searched are

Business/Finance	13
Social Sciences	12
Current Events	11
Education/Psychology	10
Biological Sciences	5
Medical/Health Sciences	3
Engineering/Technology	2
Physical Sciences	2

Administration

10. The end-user search service is administered by

Coordinator of online searching	13
Other	9
Head of reference	5

11. The end-user search service is a

Permanent service	18
Pilot project	9

12. Funding comes from

General library budget	13

User fees	8
Reference department budget	3
University grant	3
Academic department allocation	3
Public services budget	2
Vendor (on loan)	2
Book budget	1
Online budget	1
Undergraduate enrichment fund	1

13. Users are charged

We do not charge users	15
A flat fee per minute	5
A flat fee per search	3
On a cost recovery basis	2
A flat fee per five minutes	1
Only if exceeds $8	1

14. Service is available

Evenings	23
Weekends	17
Daytime	9
On demand	3
Only when reference desk is staffed	2

15. Service is offered

More than 20 hours per week	11
10 to 20 hours per week	9
Less than 10 hours per week	2

16. Service is staffed by

Librarians	19
Student assistants	6
Combination of personnel	5
Support staff	4
Library school students	1
Graduate students	1
Not staffed	1

17. Hardware for the service is

Library owned	22
On loan	4
University owned	2
Rented or leased	1

18. Number of terminals available is

One	10
Two	9
Three	2
More than three	6

19. Type of equipment used is

Microcomputer	22
Printer	16
Modem	15
Dumb terminal	10

20. Location of service is

Near reference desk	14
In reference department, away from desk	11
Not in reference department	4

Experiences

21. Advantages experienced

Increased user satisfaction	20
Enhanced campus image	16
Access to current information	16
Low cost	11
Ease of use	10
Reduced librarian workload	1
Brings people to reference desk	1
Few advantages	1
User awareness of online service	1
Improved per index access	1

22. Disadvantages experienced

Increased staff workload	19
Ill-prepared users	14
Machine malfunctions	9
Restrictive results	6
Less use than expected	6
Restrictive hours	4
Downtime	3
Increased ILL activity	1
High cost	1
Difficult commands	1
Lack of training materials	1
Poorly designed software	1
Assumption/per holdings	1

23. Important variables contributing to the success of an end-user search service

User training	19
Staff training	18
Administrative support	16
Quality of software	16
Space	13
Staff acceptance	9
Publicity	9
Quality of hardware	9
Quality of documentation	2
Search lab facilities	1

| Low cost | 1 |
| Presearch counseling | 1 |

Institutional Characteristics

24. Highest degree offered

Doctorate	15
Masters	9
Baccalaureate	1

25. Average number of searchers 9

LIBRARIES SURVEYED

University of Akron
University of Arkansas, Little Rock
Bowling Green State University
Cal Poly, Pomona
California State University
    Bakersfield
    Chico
    Humboldt
    San Francisco
University of California
    Berkeley
    Davis
    San Diego
    San Francisco
    Santa Barbara
Carnegie-Mellon University
University of Cincinnati
University of Colorado, Boulder
University of Connecticut
Cornell University
University of Delaware
De Paul University
De Pauw University
Earlham College
Florida Institute of Technology
George Mason University
George Washington University
Georgetown University
Kent State University
Lehigh University
Mansfield University
Memphis State University
University of Michigan
University of Missouri, Columbia
Nazareth College of Rochester
New York University
North Carolina State University
Northern Illinois University
Northwestern University
University of Ottawa
Pennsylvania State University
Philadelphia College of Pharmacy
Purdue University

University of Rochester
Stanford University
University of Tennessee, Knoxville
Texas A&M University
University of Vermont
University of Washington
University of Wisconsin, Parkside
Willamette University

NOTES

1. Charles T. Meadow, "Online Searching and Computer Programming: Some Behavioral Similarities (Or, Why End Users Will Eventually Take Over the Terminal)," *Online* 3 (1979): 3.

2. Sarah E. Thomas, *End-User Searching Services*. Kit 122. (Washington, DC: Office of Management Studies, Association of Research Libraries, March 1986).

3. Linda Friend, "Independence at the Terminal: Training. Student End-Users to Do Online Literature Searching," *Journal of Academic Librarianship* 11 (July 1985): 140.

4. Edward G. Summer, Robert E. Bruce, and Bryan R. Clark. "Using Microcomputers to Augment a Mainframe Bibliographic Search Service: A Case Study in Developing End User Personal Information Systems," *Educational Technology* (February 1986): 26.

BIBLIOGRAPHY

Buntrock, Robert E. and Aldona Valicenti. "End-Users and Chemical Information." *Journal of Chemical Information and Computer Sciences* 25 (August 1985): 203-207.

Crooks, James. "End User Searching at the University of Michigan Library." *Proceedings of the 6th National Online Meeting*, 99-110. Medford, NJ: Learned Information, 1985.

Des Chene, Dorice. "Online Searching by End-Users." *RQ* 25 (Fall 1985): 89-95.

Dodd, Jane, Charles Gilreath, and Geraldine Hutchins. *Texas A&M University Library. A Final Report from the Public Services Research Projects*. Bethesda, MD: ERIC Document Reproduction Service, 1985. ED 255224.

Eisenberg, Michael. *The Direct Use of Online Bibliographic Information Systems by Untrained End Users: A Review of Research*. Syracuse, NY: ERIC Clearinghouse on Information Resources, 1983.

(Also available as ERIC Document ED 238440).

Fogel, Laurence and Claire F. Zigmund. "End User vs. Intermediary: A Personal Perspective." *Proceedings of the 6th National Online Meeting.* Medford, NJ: Learned Information, 1985: 153-159.

Friend, Linda. "Identifying and Informing the Potential End-User: Online Information Seminars." *Online* 10 (January 1986): 47-56.

————. "Independence at the Terminal: Training Student End-Users to Do Online Literature Searching." *Journal of Academic Librarianship* 11 (July 1985): 136-141.

Haines, Judith S. "Experience in Training End-User Searchers." *Online* 6 (November 1982): 14-23.

Halperin, Michael and Ruth A. Pagell. "Service Configurations for End-User Searching." *Database End-User* 2 (March 1986): 20-22.

Janke, Richard V. "Presearch Counseling for Client Searchers (End Users)." *Online* 9 (September 1985): 13-26.

————. "Online after Six: End User Searching Comes of Age." *Online* 8 (November 1984): 15-22.

Krueger, G.L. and D. Des Chene. "Introducing On-Line Information Retrieval to the Undergraduate and Graduate Students in Chemistry." *Journal of Chemical Education* 57 (1980): 457.

Lippincott, Joan. "Teaching End-Users to Search Online Bibliographic Databases." *Agricultural Libraries Information Notes* 9 (October 1983): 1-3.

Lucia, Joseph and Christine Roysdon. "Online Searching as an Educational Technology: Teaching Computer-Wise End-Users." *Proceedings of the 5th National Online Meeting*, 187-194. Medford, NJ: Learned Information, 1984.

Lyon, Sally. "End User Searching of Online Databases: A Selective Annotated Bibliography." *Library Hi Tech* 2 (1984): 47-60.

Machovec, George S. "The Changing Role of Librarians as End-Users become More Active Online Searches." *Information Intelligence, Online Libraries, and Microcomputers* 2 (March 1984): 1-3.

Marleski, Susan. "End-User Training: A Model for the Information Professional." *Proceedings of the Online 82 Conference*, 25-30. Weston, CT: Online, 1982.

Norris, Carol. "Online Micros: End-User Training." *Proceedings of the Small Computers in Libraries Software/Computer Conference and Exposition for Information Managers and Librarians*, 341. Westport, CT: Meckler Publishing Company, 1986.

Osegueda, Laura M. and Judy Reynolds. "Introducing Online into the University Curriculum." *RQ* 22 (Fall 1982): 17-31.

Quint, Barbara. "Question: What's an End User?" *Database End-User* 1 (September 1985): 3.

Tenopir, Carol. "Systems for End Users: Are There End Users for the Systems?" *Library Journal* 110 (15 June 1985): 40-41.

Thomas, Sarah E. *End-User Searching Services.* Kit 122. Washington, DC: Office of Management Studies, Association of Research Libraries, March 1986.

Ward, Sandra N. and Laura M. Osegueda. "Teaching University Student End-Users about Online Searching." *Science and Technology Libraries* 5 (Fall 1984): 17-31.

Woolpy, Sara and Nancy Taylor. "End-User Searching: A Study of Manual vs. Online Searching by End-Users and the Role of the Intermediary." *Proceedings of the Online 84 Conference*, 243-245. Weston, CT: Online, 1984.

Faculty as End-Users:

Strategies, Challenges, and Rewards

Susan Swords Steffen

Online searching and the need for users to learn to use online search systems independently represents the single largest change in the kind of resources librarians can provide, and in the way that research is done. The enthusiastic acceptance and instant success of online catalogs, end-user search services, and video disk search systems, wherever they are introduced, bear witness to users' desires to use new information technologies to meet information needs.

Yet, in many academic libraries, one significant user group--the faculty--seems somewhat reluctant to jump into the online age. Although no formal study of use of online search services by faculty has been done, most reports of online search activity show faculty as a relatively small user group. Informally, librarians frequently comment that faculty do not use their online search services very much.

For most faculty, online searching is a new and unknown research tool that was not available when they learned how to do research in graduate school. They are not sure how, or even why, they might want to use online searching, and so they stick with the sources familiar to them. Relying on a librarian to search requires the researcher to sacrifice his or her independence and thus substantially change his or her style of research. Many faculty have little experience with computers, are anxious about using them, and are somewhat distrustful of what they produce. Unfortunately, some faculty have had bad experiences with the results of online searches, such as the failure to produce material known to exist, poor quality of a particular database, inability to locate materials cited in a search, or high costs. It is no wonder that faculty

Steffen is the Head of Schaffner Library, Northwestern University, Chicago, IL.

have not been as wildly enthusiastic about online searching as librarians hoped.

The advent of end-user online searching provides academic libraries with a new opportunity to make online searching more accessible and more useful to faculty. By learning how to do their own online searching, faculty gain an understanding of this resource and learn how to incorporate it into their own research style and method. Faculty are more likely to make use of online search service as end-users because while doing their own searching, they are able to make optimal use of the research skills they already have, interact with the computer until they find the information most appropriate to their needs, and acquire increased confidence in the results of online searching. In short, end-user online searching allows faculty to make use of online resources without substantially changing their research style.[1]

To be effective end-users who can retrieve results that will be satisfying to them, faculty need to learn the fundamentals of search strategy formulation, the commands needed to interact with the computer, the variety of databases and the search aids available, and the options for access to online searching. These skills can be easily and effectively learned from librarians who are already expert searchers. Successful end-user instruction programs for faculty must be carefully designed to meet the needs and expectations of faculty. Today, I would like to discuss strategies to use in designing programs for faculty, methods for providing faculty access to end-user searching, and finally, the benefits that librarians and libraries may expect to enjoy from this type of instructional program.

INSTRUCTION PROGRAMS FOR FACULTY

The first step in designing instruction in online searching for faculty, as with the design of any type of instruction, is to recognize the knowledge that they bring to the task. Most faculty begin their study of online searching with little if any knowledge of the process at all. Some may have had online searches done for them, read about the tool in computer magazines or professional journals, or heard about the service from students. However, they will probably have no understanding of Boolean logic, search strategy formulation, the variety of databases available, or the use of computer equipment. Often, they are much less familiar with print equivalents of online databases and their thesauri than might be expected.

On the other hand, most faculty do possess a large variety of sophisticated research skills appropriate to their area of specialization. Posing research questions, defining and focusing topics, and locating preliminary background information about a subject do not present problems for faculty. Unlike instruction in online searching for students, which focuses on how to construct a research strategy of which online searching is a part, instruction for faculty emphasizes how online searching fits in with and enhances the research methods they already use. They need to learn to translate the skills they already have and the research style they already feel comfortable with into the language of online searching (i.e., search strategy formulation, the selection of appropriate terms, the selection of databases, and the application of Boolean logic).

Many faculty learned their research skills from their own graduate school professors or by the "discovery method" rather than through formal bibliographic instruction. Consequently, they often know less than might be expected about how bibliographic tools are organized, what they contain, and what search aids are available. Since a basic understanding of indexing practices and skill in using thesauri can greatly improve search results, faculty appreciate some discussion of these topics. This information will also assist them in doing print research, but most faculty are less likely to attend instructional programs about print resources they think they should already know about. In addition to improving their ability to do online searching, this information makes them much more aware of the richness and complexity of the information resources available today.

In addition to fulfilling their own research need, most faculty are interested in introducing new ideas and techniques to students. Throughout each presentation, it is important that faculty be shown how the needs of their students can be met through the use of online searching. Faculty members should also be made aware of the problems their students might encounter. This kind of information affords faculty the opportunity to share their newly-acquired skills with their students. Suggestions for assignments that make use of online searching and about bibliographic instruction that might make such assignments work better are also appropriate.

Fairly traditional instruction methods, such as lecture and discussion, are most effective with faculty because those are the methods they are most familiar with and probably use most often themselves. Computer-assisted instruction or relying on user-friendly software are less effective, because these methods require the faculty to use a technology that is unfamiliar. The presence of a human instructor, who can relate the process back to the familiar academic world and act as an ally and colleague, is important in encouraging the acceptance of this new technology. Handouts to take notes on and to keep for future reference are very important.

Like most end-users, faculty will probably not search frequently enough to remember all the necessary commands. They will need something as a reference to refresh their memories in the future.

An essential element in online search training for faculty is hands-on practice time with a coach. This practice time should be on one of the major daytime search systems, such as DIALOG or BRS, because faculty frequently need access to the full range of databases to meet their research needs. If they cannot find materials of interest to them, they quickly become skeptical about online searching. Seeing the results of a successful online search on a topic of interest is essential to the acceptance of online searching by faculty. A coach is necessary for help in formulating the final search strategy, for dealing with the computer, and for making further refinements to the search during the process. Faculty often want to do sophisticated searching (e.g., searching in multiple databases, limiting by date, looking for work done at a particular institution); they will need some help in conducting their first search.

Many faculty are quite anxious about using computers, and even those that have made some use of computers have probably not used as sophisticated and complex an application as online searching, and not with the "meter running." In fact, some faculty participate in online searching workshops to help them overcome their fear of computers and to become more computer literate. Emphasizing research strategy and topic formulation while discussing the search commands needed for interacting with the computer helps to alleviate this computer anxiety. Providing separate training for faculty away from students enables the instructor and the faculty to discuss this uneasiness about technology openly. Any problems related to equipment should be mentioned, but de-emphasized as much as possible. For the computer anxious, hands-on practice time will be a computer literacy exercise as well as online search practice time, and an understanding coach can do much to put them at their ease and make this a positive experience.

In addition to an understanding of online searching skills, faculty need information about the options they have for getting access to online searching. They need information about the organization of the online world, about establishing their own accounts with online vendors, about the equipment required, and about using library equipment and passwords. They also need to be well-versed in their students' options including services available, instruction available, and costs.

Providing instructional programs for faculty end-users is not without problems. It is a labor intensive activity that is not only time-consuming, but, like much teaching, very demanding. Adding another instructional activity to already over-committed librarians may be difficult. Good instructional materials for faculty are not available, and developing them is expensive in terms of time and money. Regardless of the quality of the program offered, such training efforts will never reach the number of users that efforts oriented to students will. It is important to measure the success of such programs in terms other than the numbers served. Most faculty have extremely busy and complicated schedules; arranging workshops when people can come and insuring that they actually attend requires a great deal of persistent effort. Often, it is not possible to arrange for faculty to attend by subject area, and so each group is a mix of scientists, humanists, and social scientists who will need to use different databases in different ways. While faculty seem to enjoy the diversity in the group, this mix makes finding good illustrative examples and including information relevant for everyone challenging. Finally, costs for practice time must be covered either by participants, the library, or some other source. While the availability of DIALOG classroom passwords and the BRS INSTRUCTOR program for use with faculty keeps training costs low, at least one half-hour of practice per participant should be available and must be paid for.

OPTIONS FOR PROVIDING FACULTY ACCESS TO SEARCHING

Facilitating faculty access to online searching can be quite simple or quite involved, requiring a great deal of commitment from a library or very little. At the very least, participants can be provided with information about arranging for individual passwords with vendors; consultation on search strategy may also be offered with relatively little effort. As another consultant service, the library's collection of search aids can be made publicly available for faculty to consult in preparing search strategies or prior to purchase. Books about online searching, particularly the type designed for end-users, can be added to a library's collection.

A significant number of faculty will probably need access to search equipment as well as passwords because they will be only occasional users. If time permits, faculty may be allowed to use library search equipment and library passwords, and then be billed for time used. Another option would be to subsidize all or part of searching costs. Some libraries are setting up separate end-user search facilities for students or are making end-user searching available in microcomputer labs located in the library. While these student facilities may also be made available to faculty for end-user searching, some faculty may not feel comfortable searching in a room full of students. A facility designed especially for faculty may meet their needs better. Other libraries are cooperating with computer facilities available on their campuses to provide training in and/or access to online searching outside the library.

Another option, one that is currently being implemented at Northwestern University's Medical Library, is for a library to act as a broker for passwords. Faculty can sign up for BRS/COLLEAGUE and KNOWLEDGE INDEX passwords through the library at a discounted rate. Usage on these is then billed on one invoice to the library, and the library bills the individual users. The library provides training and consultation services and is able to monitor the use of searching among its users. Users get a discounted searching rate and a simplified billing procedure. Without this arrangement, the library feels it would lose its role as information center for the medical school as more and more faculty would begin doing business directly with the vendors.

BENEFITS TO LIBRARIANS AND LIBRARIES

The rewards of providing training in online searching to faculty far outweigh any problems encountered. In this period of over-extended public services staffs, changing roles and expectations, and ever-expanding information technology, entering into another new labor intensive activity may seem imprudent. However, the benefits experienced by librarians and libraries are potentially so great that the effort should be made.

Increasingly, academic librarians are being called upon to reassess their traditional roles, to adopt new ones, and to act as "research colleagues, bibliographic experts, information system managers, and information system use instructors."[2] Reference librarians in particular are urged to shift their role from question-answerer and information provider to teacher and consultant.[3] For the past twenty years, librarians involved in BI have been working hard to establish themselves as teachers, but on many campuses this is still an uphill battle that has not yet been won. Training faculty to do their own online searching is not only consistent with these roles, but it also enhances them.

First, the experience of learning how to do online searching from a librarian allows faculty to observe a librarian as a teacher and an information consultant, two roles of a librarian that are unfamiliar to most faculty. In my experience teaching faculty, even faculty who had been previously involved in a very active bibliographic instruction program reported that they perceived me to be more of a teacher because I was teaching something that they did not know and wanted to learn. Faculty trained in searching have a much greater appreciation of librarians' online searching skills than those who have not received training (who seem to regard the process as something just short of magic), and are much more likely to seek consultation from a librarian on the selection of databases and the formulation of search strategies.

Second, many librarians are not yet completely comfortable with the new roles they are being asked to assume, and will benefit from some positive experiences in carrying them out. Giving instruction in online searching to faculty provides librarians with an opportunity to "try on" the roles of teacher and consultant with a well-defined group of users who will respond positively to their efforts. By acting as a consultant to faculty who are constructing their own search strategies, librarians can learn how to give advice without actually conducting the search.

Third, even librarians actively involved in bibliographic instruction programs will improve their teaching skills. Although teaching library skills is one of the major activities of many reference librarians, much of this teaching consists of one-hour lectures and does not go beyond a fairly basic level; it is frequently directed to unwilling or at least fairly disinterested audiences. The more sophisticated content of end-user training requires more thought and planning and thus, provides a good opportunity to improve teaching skills. Faculty make enthusiastic students who are excited about the subject and interested in learning, which can be a tremendous morale booster to librarians who are accustomed to many sections of basic freshman bibliographic instruction. Improved teaching skills will also increase librarians' confidence as teachers, and make them more amenable to involvement in other instructional programs.

Finally, when faculty and librarians have a clearer understanding of the instructional role of librarians, even bibliographic instruction programs for students experience important benefits. Participating in an instruction program themselves seems to be remarkably effective in convincing faculty of the value of instruction in information retrieval skills. Many faculty simply cannot imagine what a librarian would talk about for a whole hour or how it could benefit the class since they have never had this experience. Students will increasingly need to learn about the use of online sources, and faculty who are knowledgeable about, rather than threatened by, these resources will be more likely to incorporate appropriate assignments into their courses. Faculty who become "converts" often want their students to have experience with online searching. Faculty who are reluctant to include bibliographic instruction in their courses, because they feel students should already know how to do research, may be more amenable to including online searching instruction because no one is reasonably expected to already know this.

Past bibliographic instruction experiences have convincingly demonstrated that when faculty and librarians collaborate in bibliographic instruction, these efforts are the most successful. Librarians can only work as colleagues with faculty who regard them as fellow teachers with valuable knowledge. Faculty who are knowledgeable about online searching and about the librarians' skills can work closely with librarians as equals to design appropriate assignments, prepare students for searches, and even jointly conduct searches. Positive attitude and enthusiasm from faculty are the most effective means of motivating students to learn this new skill.

Just as individual librarians and faculty members are struggling with new roles, so are academic libraries struggling with re-defining their mission. While helping a significant and often powerful group of users meet their information needs more effectively, training in online searching for faculty establishes the library as a center for instruction in the use of, for information about, and for access to information technology. If libraries do not firmly establish this as part of their mission and keep control of their information center function, other units within institutions, perhaps centralized in computer centers or decentralized in the various departments, may assume parts of this function. Researchers may come to rely less and less on the library, and its position will be eroded. Changing the faculty's perception of these roles promotes them as advocates for the library in the campus community where faculty spokespersons can be much more effective than librarians in arguing the case.

While it is surely overstating the case to say that these critical problems in the future of academic librarians and libraries can be completely solved simply by providing faculty with training in online searching, such programs can make an important and valuable contribution toward their solutions. Knowledgeable faculty members, who

confidently and competently use online resources and who have experienced librarians acting as teachers and consultants, will be powerful allies in the introduction of new programs and services and in the reallocation of resources. The perceptions of a significant group of library users about librarians and libraries will be changed, librarians will be better prepared to meet the challenges of the future, and libraries will have reaffirmed their role as the information center for the academic community. At the same time, libraries will be helping a significant group of users meet their information needs in a way that is comfortable for and useful to them, now and in the future-- which, after all, is what libraries are all about.

NOTES

1. For a more extensive discussion of faculty motivation for attending and response to an end-user training program see: Susan Swords Steffen, "College Faculty Goes Online: Training Faculty End Users," *Journal of Academic Librarianship* 12 (July 1986): 147-151. Other discussions of programs for faculty include: Alice Bodtke-Roberts, "Faculty End-User Searching of BIOSIS." In *Proceedings of the Fourth National Online Meeting, 12-14 April, 1983*, 45-56 (New York: Learned Information, 1983). Linda Friend, "Identifying and Informing the Potential End User: Online Information Seminars." *Online* (January 1986): 47-56. Clyde W. Grotophorst, "Training University Faculty as End-User Searchers: A CAI Approach." In *Proceedings of the Fifth National Online Meeting, 10-12 April 1984*, 77-82. (New York: Learned Information, 1984).

2. Allen B. Veaner, "1985 to 1995: The Next Decade in Academic Librarianship, Part I," *College and Research Libraries* 46 (May 1985): 209-229. See especially p.217.

3. "Replacing the Fast Fact Drop-In with Gourmet Information Service: A Symposium," *Journal of Academic Librarianship* 11 (May 1985): 68-78.

Integrating Online Searching into

Traditional Bibliographic Instruction

Scott Stebelman

This presentation addresses how online literature searching can be integrated into traditional library instruction. It is based on my library instruction activities at the University of Nebraska-Lincoln, and my observations of the instructional program at George Washington University, where I have recently joined the staff. Nebraska's library follows a strict subject specialist model, where the library liaison for a teaching department is also responsible for satisfying the library instruction and online searching needs of that department; GWU's library follows a generalist model, with each librarian in the reference department providing instruction and searching for a wide variety of disciplines and departments.

The assumption underlying the subject specialist model is that the people who have the strongest backgrounds, or training in an area, will be most knowledgeable about the research tools and databases for that area. A librarian with a masters degree or doctorate in a discipline will be aware of the argot, methodology, major authorities, and developing trends within it, and will be able to pass on this detailed understanding to users. Moreover, because he or she will have daily contact with the specialized research tools within the discipline, they--just like a physician prescribing the correct drug from among thousands--will know which tool to prescribe for a variety of researchers within the discipline. An additional reason for subject specialists to concentrate their instruction and searching in their departments is pragmatic: the best way to establish strong liaison relationships with a department is to be the exclusive provider of vital library services, such as instruction and online searching. A symbiotic

Stebelman is BI/Reference Librarian, Gelman Library, George Washington University, Washington, DC.

relationship ultimately develops between the librarian and his/her academic department: as the department becomes increasingly dependent on the specialist to provide these services, so the specialist becomes increasingly dependent on the department to maintain his or her subject expertise, by channeling students and faculty to them.

In contrast to Nebraska, GWU did not develop a subject specialist model until 1985, when selection responsibilities shifted from the faculty to the library. Although the subject specialists have been selecting books according to subject responsibilities, there has been no corresponding allocation of instructional or online search responsibilities, at least at the undergraduate level. Subject specialists will provide advanced instruction to graduate students and faculty in their area, but undergraduate instruction is provided by the librarian who is free at the scheduled time and has an interest in the topic. Online searching, with the exception of the sciences, is administered in the same manner: patrons determine the most convenient time for their searches, and the librarian on duty at that time executes the search.

Both Nebraska and GWU use a workbook to teach basic information retrieval skills to undergraduates. Administered through the English Department, the workbook trains students to use the card catalog, periodical indexes, and other tools to locate information and materials on pre-assigned subjects. At Nebraska, no end-user systems were available to students; thus all online searching was conducted by librarians. The same held true for GWU until 1986, when BRS/After Dark was offered to students, who could choose either a librarian to do the search or, after brief instruction, do the search themselves. Because of the reduced nightly cost, searching is within the reach of most students (GWU charges patrons $5 for 15 minutes of connect time). Given the lower rates and the growing importance online searching is assuming in research, GWU is exploring the feasibility of incorporating an end-user search unit into the workbook. The computer would be viewed no differently than any other reference tool: its function would be to generate bibliographies, verify citations, and provide factual information to students. One of the fears many librarians have about online searching is that it undermines traditional library instruction--students paying librarians to find relevant articles on term paper topics. However, if students were to become responsible for their own searches, they would also have to become responsible for search preparation. In preparing for these searches, students, like librarians, would learn the idiosyncrasies of their databases, such as vocabulary control, document types indexed, time coverage of the databases, and any special

features. In the process, the students would become better informed not only about online searching but about how information in more conventional tools is organized and accessed.

Even though workbooks are an effective way of teaching basic skills to a large number of students, staff re-allocations or budgetary constraints may require their suspension. When this happened at Nebraska, workbooks were replaced by tours and workshops, where students learned about specific tools and research strategies that would help them write their papers. The instruction included much of the material covered in the workbook, but whenever time permitted a visit was made to the computer search room. First the service was explained, then students were asked what topics they could be writing on; at that point an actual search would be conducted, to see how many citations could be found on one or two of the topics. While the computer was searching and posting the terms, a quick overview of online searching was given to the students, explaining that databases usually corresponded to print indexes, that they were often more current than their print counterparts, and that specific elements in a citation (e.g., author, journal name) could be searched more efficiently by the computer than by hand. Students were then provided with a directory of subject specialists, and told that if they wanted a search conducted, they should contact the appropriate librarian. Nothing sells a service like immediate need, and shortly thereafter several of the students returned to have their topics searched. Many of the pedagogical concerns, mentioned earlier, arose in this context: how much learning occurred if librarians compiled the students' bibliographies? Two values were in conflict here--the belief that students not only needed to know, but had the right to know, about the latest information technology, and the belief that students, as incipient scholars, needed to become self-reliant in using libraries.

In addition to those provided for undergraduates, workshops were given to graduate students and faculty.[1] Graduate students were easy to reach through the Methods of Scholarship course, which they were strongly encouraged to take. Again, as with the undergraduates, online searching was presented as one research strategy among many. Particularly successful was discussing online searching in the context of citation indexing; citation indexing is still a novel concept to many humanists, who use standard bibliographies, serendipity, and footnotes to identify relevant literature. Given the complexity of the ISI indexes, online searching eliminates much of the confusion patrons experience in shifting from the different volumes. Another advantage that online searching has at these workshops is to show the ease with which interdisciplinary research

QUESTIONS ABOUT COMPUTERIZED LITERATURE SEARCHING

1. What topics are best searched by a computer?
   A. Those topics or terms that have limited denotations or are stock concepts (for example, "character traits" is so broad a term that we could list several hundred examples; "pride" or "hubris" are narrow enough conceptually that more words would be unnecessary).
   B. Those topics that are multidisciplinary and require checking several databases (examples: "Utopian Philosophy in 18th Century Europe"; "Piaget and the Development of Writing Skills").

2. What are the advantages of searching by a computer?
   A. It is much faster than a manual search, often taking seconds to scan thousands of citations.
   B. Citations and abstracts are printed out for you.
   C. More fields within a citation are accessible by a computer. You can search, and limit, to a particular journal, time period, language, publication format (e.g., articles only), and others.
   D. With the exception of the *MLA Bibliography*, databases are more up-to-date than their print counterparts. Updates are often done monthly or quarterly.
   E. The same topic can be searched automatically every time a new computer tape is entered into the database.
   F. Some companies will provide photocopies of all articles cited (for a charge).
   G. Some databases are not available in print, such as *ABI Inform* (a business index).

3. Disadvantages
   A. The computer is intellectually inflexible--it will search *only* those terms you tell it to.
   B. Often the same database covers a shorter time span than the printed index. For example, the *National Newspaper Index*, which indexes the *New York Times, Wall Street Journal*, and *Christian Science Monitor*, is searchable only from 1979.
   C. Computers cannot distinguish relevant from irrelevant word contexts. For example, if you were searching "Black Dialects," and told the computer to search any variant of "speaking" and "black," you might get "Black Elk Speaks: An Analysis

of Folk Structure." Computers are also insensitive to the metaphorical use of language. If you were researching Milton's blindness and asked the computer to search "Milton" and "blindness," you could get an article entitled, "Milton's Blindness to Patristic Heresies."

4. What is the cost of a search?
   A. It all depends on what database(s) you want searched and how many citations you want printed. The *MLA Bibliography* costs $1.08 a minute to search, *Historical Abstracts* $1.25, and ERIC $.58 a minute. Citations can run from $.05 to $.30 each, depending on how much information is in the citation (e.g., author, title, volume number, and date; descriptors; notes; and abstracts) you want printed. Also, the more databases you want searched, the greater the cost. Most searches in the humanities run between $5 and $15; the library will subsidize $75 a year for faculty searches and $20 for one search by a Ph.D. candidate.

5. When can I expect to receive the results?
   If you only need citations without abstracts, they can be printed at the time of the search. If you are searching a database that has abstracts, it is cheaper to have them printed offline; on those occasions it will take four or five days to come through the mail from California (where the computer is located).

6. Additional databases relevant to literary research:
   A. *America: History and Life* (1963-)
   B. *Historical Abstracts* (1973-)
   C. *Philosopher's Index* (1940-)
   D. *RILM* (music; 1971-78)
   E. *ERIC* (education; 1966-)
   F. *Language Abstracts* (1973-)
   G. *ArtBibliographies Modern* (art history, nineteenth and twentieth centuries, 1974-)
   H. *Religion Index* (time period varies for monographs and periodicals)
   I. *Arts & Humanities Citation Index* (1975-)

7. Whom should I contact for a search?
   Scott Stebelman, 217 Love Library, ext. 2525.

can be facilitated through computers. Taking a topic such as "Religion and the Victorian Idea of Progress," a searcher can draw citations from *Religion Index, Historical Abstracts, Dissertations Abstracts, Sociological Abstracts,* and other databases. Although the librarian can emphasize the role of computers in interdisciplinary research, a point that is rarely lost on the faculty is the unique role of the librarian in facilitating the research. The librarian, aware of interdisciplinary databases, is also aware of nonemclature/descriptor changes that exist in different disciplines and that may have escaped the faculty.

Although many Nebraska faculty attended workshops presented at the library, many others did not, either because of inertia or because of professional skepticism. To counter these problems, it was useful at times to provide instruction on their turf rather than the library's. This meant advertising workshops several weeks in advance, bringing a modem and portable terminal over to the departmental lounge, connecting a telephone to the modem, and taking faculty requests on demand. For those faculty who did not attend the workshops, a visit was made--terminal in hand--to their offices and searches executed at their desks. This allowed bibliographies on their favorite research topic to be printed instantaneously, and provided an opportunity to suggest additional tools that might expedite the research. Because subject specialists did selection for the department as well as searching, these sessions also provided information about any new research and curricular interests the faculty might have, for which additional library materials could be purchased.

In discussing the heavy search load at Nebraska, it must be stressed that online searching is subsidized, up to $75 a year, for the faculty, and up to $20 for Ph.D. candidates. This eliminates the financial risk and loss these patrons otherwise would incur; it also explains why the vast bulk of computer searches are done for these two groups, in contrast to many other campuses, where undergraduate volume is greater. At Nebraska, the number of searches for 1984 and 1985 was 2,542; at GWU, which has no subsidy and a smaller student body, the number was 305.

Many undergraduate students, growing up with video games and having had some computer training in primary and secondary schools, are less impressed with the novelty of computerized searching than are many older librarians. In some cases, we have to demystify the process for ourselves and view it as any other research tool or service we make available to patrons. By integrating online searching into traditional undergraduate instruction, we expose students to state-of-the-art retrieval systems, reinforce that those retrieval systems are not limited to, but extend beyond libraries, and provide them with additional research tools that may enhance the quality of their papers. For those librarians who do online searching as part of their departmental liaison function, the database and cross-disciplinary expertise they bring to the interviews enhance their professional status with the faculty and often leads to increased instructional opportunities.

NOTE

1. The author, as subject specialist for English and American literature at Nebraska, provided most of his instruction to the English department.

Teaching End-Users to Search:

Issues and Problems

David N. King with **Betsy Baker**

To have a working title like "Issues and Problems," enables you to talk on just about anything you want. On the other hand, particularly in a program like this year's LOEX conference, where so many discussions and presentations focus on a relatively circumscribed topic, there is the risk of simply reiterating what others have already said. The issues and problems that our speakers have identified so far are real, practical issues and real, practical problems that anyone concerned with teaching end-users to search will have to face. I have decided, however, not to offer an itemized list of those same issues and problems, as important as they are. Instead, at the risk of being perceived as a "library school type" more concerned with principles and theory than "real world" library practice, I would like to address what I see as some of the more fundamental issues and problems that we face--issues and problems that I think are at the heart of many practical problems mentioned by our previous speakers. I am relieved, in a way, that these fundamental problems have not been the topic of much discussion yet, because it gives me something to say. However, I cannot help feeling a bit surprised that what I see as "fundamental" has not yet been dealt with at length. Perhaps surprised is not the right word, because the neglect of these issues is endemic in all professions and every segment of our society, not just librarianship. Though the specifics may differ, anyone today who is grappling with newer technologies is facing crises of knowledge and practice. We are certainly not alone.

I do not think it is unfair to characterize the current state of affairs in librarianship as a

King is with Graduate School of Library and Information Science University of Illinois, Urbana, IL and **Baker** is BI Services Librarian, Northwestern University Library, Evanston, IL.

state of crisis. Most may prefer to refer to it as a period of transition, as we maneuver to integrate and adapt to the new information technologies. But what we decide and what we do, today and tomorrow, shapes our future as a profession, and the library's future as an institution. Every decision and every action--and every decision not to act--is critical. Ideally, the actions we take should be founded upon knowledge. Yet, for many of us here today (including myself), and for many in our profession, what we *don't* know about information technology and its use far exceeds what we *do* know. What we *thought* we knew, we have often found we were wrong about. More and more, we are coming to realize that what we *do* know is just how much we *don't* know; and when it comes to technology, if knowledge is power, then ignorance is, at the very least, expensive.

Since ignorance is my biggest problem, I am going to talk about things this morning that I know nothing about. Since there are other people who also admit they have a lot to learn about these things, and *they* are experts, perhaps I should tell you what they think as well. I should warn you that some of this falls into that vague category commonly referred to as "theory," because however important it may be, it is not really the "nuts-and-bolts, how-to" of library practice. For those of you who might want to blame my return to library school for this, I assure you that (much to the chagrin and frustration of former colleagues on the practical front of librarianship) I have always been like this--looking for underlying explanations for what we do and why. Better judgment did catch up with me this morning, however. I had threatened to discuss ten of these fundamental problems, as Carolyn mentioned when she introduced me. But knowing that a little of this goes a long way for many people, I would like to concentrate on just three, and try to indicate along the way how these three problem areas affect the nuts-and-bolts of teaching end-users to search.

THE NATURE OF TECHNOLOGY AND TECHNOLOGY-USE

The first problem, and the most fundamental one to me, has to do with the term "technology." Definitions are as basic as it gets. Most people think of technology as things--tools, particularly *new* tools. We often use the word technology to encompass a group of tools, such as computers and optical disks, and other information processing and communication devices. Sometimes we use the plural and talk about "technologies" as a way of grouping different types of tools that have

characteristics in common--usually their purpose or their design features.

If we look instead at the definitions of technology, we find a much different meaning. For example, John Kenneth Galbraith, in *The New Industrial State*,[1] defines technology as "the systematic application of scientific or other organized knowledge to practical tasks." You find much the same sort of definition in the *OED* and *Webster's Unabridged*. Others, like Arnold Pacey whose book, *The Culture of Technology*, is one of the most readable and significant in recent years, have expanded Galbraith's definition to express the real breadth and scope of technology. For example, "technology is the systematic application of scientific or other organized knowledge to practical tasks by ordered systems that involve people and organizations, living things and machines" and other tools.[2] This type of definition is so broad as to be almost more than we can easily conceptualize. Perhaps you understand it differently than I, but I interpret it to mean, not only that a card catalog is just as much technology as an online catalog, but also that everything we do as librarians and every tool we create or use in our professional endeavors, insofar as it involves technology; that libraries are, and always have been, technological enterprises; maybe even that the library *itself*, to the extent that it is a tool for the storage and retrieval of information by users, is technology.

However innocuous this distinction between common usage of the term and its broader meaning seems, it has some very practical results in the "real world" of library practice. The broad definition sees technology as a human endeavor, individually and in concert as organizations, intended to achieve goals and fulfill needs--using inanimate tools to help attain those ends. Common usage, on the other hand, focuses on the inanimate tool, on hardware and software. Common usage reduces technology to mechanical and technical terms. It reflects and reinforces a mechanical view of the world in general, and what we do in particular. It fosters the notion that everything we do can be described and explained in cause-and-effect terms, step-by-step procedures, and linear processes. This is, after all, how machines function, and we tend to view the operation of the universe and everything in it as mechanical.[3] It is all very scientific. In online searching, we enter our terms and give our commands according to a particular pre-specified linear pattern, the system does its electronic thing according to its linear step-by-step programs, and we get our results organized in a nice linearly organized printout. Since almost everyone in modern society shares in common a mechanical world view--understands this cause-and-effect, step-by-step, linear process on at least a basic level--it is relatively easy to learn and easy to teach. It is easy to outline the mechanics of searching and the use of the equipment, and most anyone who pays attention and practices a little finds it easy to learn this aspect of searching.

Back in the old days, it was thought that the information retrieval systems being developed at that time were going to be used by those we now refer to as "end-users," not intermediaries. Among the earliest of the systems was MEDLARS and F.W. Lancaster, who was at that time involved in evaluating the system, and among the first to examine how end-users fared in searching. Even then, long before so-called "user-friendly" software made its debut, he found that most searchers had little difficulty with basic commands and system features.[4] After all, even in a command-driven system, there are not many commands to learn.

The ACRL Bibliographic Instruction Section Computer Concerns Committee has recently been involved in examining the documentation provided by vendors to new subscribers to user-friendly services. Many of you are probably familiar with these and know that the major emphasis is on the mechanics of searching. Vendors know what Lancaster discovered and what those of us who have been trying to teach users to search have found--that teaching the procedures for searching (the step-by-step process of searching) is easy. What Lancaster found, and what many of us have experienced, is that users encounter the greatest difficulties in three areas: 1) conceptualization and formalization of their information need, 2) development of a search strategy that exploits the interactiveness of an online system, and 3) selection of terminology, especially in regard to controlled vocabulary.

These are difficult for users to learn and difficult for us to teach because they are non-mechanical, non-linear processes. We can tell users to break their information need into concepts and try to think about how others might have discussed the issues, we can give them examples of how to select appropriate entry points and terminology, we can break out that old standby, the Venn diagram, and give them worksheets with columns for listing terms, we can discuss Boolean operators as mechanisms for expressing and explaining concepts to the system, and so on. But, we cannot provide a generic, step-by-step scheme that students can use for the mental processes involved in thinking out the problem. Thought is a relational, not a linear, activity.

This is also evident in the selection of terminology. Think about what you do mentally when posed a reference question that you have not encountered before. In a non-linear, complex way, the mind starts exploring the entire knowledge base with which we work--sometimes focusing on specific points of information, sometimes expanding or toying with broader concepts, sometimes going into a sort of "controlled drift" or unfocusing. Researchers do not really understand very well the way in which mental problem solving occurs or how to describe the thought process. Many are beginning to reject the information-processing models that grew out of our work with computers. Many of them feel that current descriptions, however complex, are unsatisfactory because of the relational nature of problem solving.[5]

The same situation can be seen in respect to search strategy and the searching process. Actually, quite a lot of research has been done in this area, which has culminated in a number of models of the search process. One is the familiar "building blocks" model, which entails breaking a topic into subtopics, each worked on independently during the search. The results from these subtopic searches are pulled together at the end of the search to solve the search problem. Another model, sometimes referred to as "culturing a pearl," involves finding a single good reference on the search topic, then searching for more items that are "like" the first one. In all, there have been five such models described.[6] None of them individually serves as an adequate explanation of what is, in essence, a highly relational interactive process.

The fact is, we do not really know what it is we do when we search--at least in any way that we can outline for others. We *do* it, and we often do it well. We are often very good at identifying the appropriate terminology and at conceptualizing and breaking down the information problems we encounter both at the reference desk and at the terminal. But it is, in great part, a highly creative process, which we do well, possibly, because it is that which defines the art of librarianship. And, I suspect that until we have a better understanding of how we do it, we will not be truly successful at teaching others how to do it. I doubt that this will come about anytime soon. But in the interim, we should resist the temptation to think of searching as a linear, step-by-step process that is best taught as a mechanical procedure. We should explore ways to teach our users to think about their information needs and develop the problem solving skills necessary for searching. The mechanics of searching should play a minor role in our educational efforts.

HUMAN-MACHINE RELATIONSHIPS

The second problem area I want to address this morning involves the psychological aspects of human-machine relationships. These are important because they have strong implications for the way in which information retrieval systems are used, how users learn to search, and how successful they are at searching. Sherry Turkle suggests that there may be two very different kinds of human-computer relationships, and I suspect they would also apply to other types of systems used for information retrieval.[7]

The first sort of relationship is that of master-to-tool. For some persons, the computer is simply a machine to be commanded and controlled. Computer commands are a way of coaxing the machine to respond with the desired results. The interaction with the system is inanimate and under the control of the searcher. Most librarians and experienced searchers probably maintain this sort of relationship with information retrieval systems. Most of us understand, at least in a general way, what is happening when we enter commands to search for particular terms, and why we get the responses we do. We understand enough about how records are created, and why we do certain things to retrieve those records.

The second type of human-computer relationship suggested by Turkle is anthropomorphic--the user ascribes human characteristics to the machine. Online systems, because of their interactiveness, their increasing user-friendliness, and their question-answer command-response dialogue, tend to be perceived as proxy-human. This type of relationship may be more common among those less familiar with the system, to whom the dialogue appears to have a feel of spontaneity, and who really do not understand what the system is doing when they search. New and infrequent users of information retrieval systems may tend to anthropomorphize the system. Even if they do not, however, it is probably a mistake to assume that users, especially students and inexperienced users, relate to the systems in the same way that we do. Their idea of what the computer is doing and why probably bears little resemblance to ours before they gain familiarity with the system.

Perhaps the most important result of anthropomorphizing systems is the tendency among those who do so to relinquish control of the dialogue to the computer. With new or inexperienced users, this may be a common attribute even if they do not anthropomorphize the system, since they may be unsure of the information-seeking process in general and the role of the system in particular. This obviously affects how effectively they can use the system. Some of those who anthropomorphize the system, who feel that the interaction involves loss of control, may have a negative response or, more likely, find the search process unproductive. New and inexperienced users, even if they do not anthropomorphize the computer, may find it difficult to assert authority over the system or establish a working relationship with it. Others, of course, may enjoy the proxy-human relationship and apparent spontaneity of the dialogue, experiencing the search process as one of friendly discussion.

Users more familiar with computers, but without information retrieval experience, may take a master-to-tool stance toward the system. They may enjoy the sense of power and control over sophisticated and complex systems, relishing the contest of overcoming limitations. Some of these may join that group of active, long-term, end-user searchers who want to know more and more. Others who begin with this master-to-tool stance may have a negative or unsuccessful experience, however. This is particularly true if they are first introduced to information retrieval systems with poorly designed user-friendly software. They may find the pseudo-human dialogue and repetitious menus of the system cumbersome or annoying, and may respond with impatience or exaggerate the limitations of the system.

We just do not understand very well all the psychological aspects of human-machine relationships and how they affect searching. There are those who come to us with prior experience with other types of interactive systems or previously formed opinions about newer technological products. There are those for whom "new" and "computer" automatically mean "better"--who are positively predisposed to high tech marvels, and who assess value on criteria far removed from actual utility. User accessible systems may attract this group, many of whom might never have entered the library otherwise. And there are, of course, those who cling to the familiar, who resist newer tools as unnecessary, complex, or too flashy--who will not invest the time or effort to familiarize themselves with the systems, just as others will not invest the time or effort to learn about manual tools. Some of our most experienced library users, and some among our own ranks, may resist online systems; some of our faculty fall into this group. Those who are knee-jerk high techers may ascribe to online systems more power and credibility than is justified, waiting in line to use a terminal rather than use the print equivalent of the tool shelved next to it. Those who are more rooted in the old ways may ignore the increased power now available to them, laboring through manual tools when an online search could accomplish the task in a fraction of the time.

Until we are better able to understand and identify the various manifestations of human-machine relationships, we will not be able to design instruction that is flexible enough to accommodate our diverse clientele. We will have difficulty optimizing our instructional techniques to meet their varying needs. In the meantime, we should probably explore different approaches to instruction for different groups, offering several different kinds and levels of instruction and attempting to identify those characteristics of various types of users that merit different forms of instruction. We should, at least, be cautious that we do not fall into the trap of presenting one, generic, instructional unit to all users, and most certainly we should not depend *solely* upon a few handouts and point-of-use instruction by reference librarians if we take our educational responsibilities seriously.

USER-FRIENDLY SOFTWARE

The third problem area that I want to discuss this morning is intertwined with the other two, but deserves closer attention. The technical aspects of system and software design have a great impact, of course, upon the amount of knowledge required by users to do basic searches. Without trying to address all of the inherent problems associated with system design, let me just focus on one. Some comment on the tradeoffs prevalent in systems intended for public use have important implications that should not be overlooked. Most of these tradeoffs occur as a result of the attempt to design software that is user-friendly.

Hidden in the design philosophy of much user-friendly software is the belief that it is necessary to sacrifice search and retrieval power, which might require more knowledge on the user's part, for simplicity of use. Some improvements have been made in the last few years; we are now less likely to see software that has absolutely no provision for Boolean searching. Nonetheless, there persists the notice that menu-driven systems, for example, are *inherently* more user-friendly than command-driven systems, and that Boolean searching is not really easy enough to be considered user-friendly. As a result, one suspects that, even if natural language, command-driven searching is possible with a particular software package, many users never explore the potential of information retrieval because they may never get beyond the menus. Without instruction in methods for using the power of the system and advice about the designed-in limitations of the user-friendly menus, many users may never know what the real potential and value of the system may be. This may be particularly true if their sole source of instruction is vendor documentation.

On the surface, most user-friendly software is deceptively simple, with its menus, question-answer dialogue, and listings of retrieved items. The process by which the system derives its results is completely opaque. Users have no way of knowing what the system did, what sort of designed-in limitations are at work, or what factors may have shaped the results. The invisibility of the decision processes the system uses, and the lack of transparency of the system, create a "black box." The searcher is forced to believe blindly in the results emanating from that box. There is little the user can do to analyze or challenge the processes or results. Consequently, as Leigh Estabrook points out, users may obtain less than they should have using a different tool, and believe in the quality of their search even more.[8] Since we are familiar with the control and power of natural language searching, *we* often do not trust the results of searches on user-friendly systems. Users have less experience upon which to judge the results they obtain. We may rightfully question, I think, whether it is in the best interest of our users (or to ourselves in the long run)--whether it is really "friendly"--to place our users in such a situation.

In the use of any online system, but particularly those that feature the most basic user-friendly software, users may lose contact with the overall information-searching process. With manual tools, systematic and diverse approaches to problem solving and information gathering are more obviously visible and more easily judged by the user as to their effectiveness. Choices about access points and search strategy require deliberate attention. Choices about which items to pursue and which to reject are under greater control in manual systems that in online ones that make many of those choices for the user, according to criteria that the user may not be aware of. The choices and processes used in manual searching are more open to self-review and self-criticism by the user. Such self-analysis is less feasible with online information retrieval, especially for inexperienced or infrequent users, due to system opacity.

Perhaps more insidious is the fact that such systems encourage users to think of information-seeking according to an inflexible, linear pattern. Researchers have discovered this to be surprisingly common even among search intermediaries with many years of searching experience, who rely almost invariably upon the most simple commands, techniques, and strategies.[9] Since searchers may be encouraged to think of information-seeking in linear, step-by-step terms, they may also be led to think of the world of knowledge in a one-dimensional linear way, rather than relationally. They may tend to isolate *information* from its much broader *knowledge*-base--to lose sight of the inter-relatedness of all knowledge. As a consequence, the pursuit of isolated bits of information may replace the pursuit of knowledge. This bodes ill, not only for the future of scholarship, but also for a society already suffering the repercussions of overspecialization.

Of course, this tendency to partition knowledge

into segments, each handled bibliographically by separate tools is nothing new to online databases. Our printed tools do much the same thing. But much of our bibliographic instruction efforts in recent years have discarded the tool-specific approaches to teaching information-seeking. There is a greater risk, perhaps, with online systems. If users do tend to concentrate, not only on online information-seeking rather than judicious use of online and manual tools, but on one or a few specific databases with which they are familiar, their approach to information-seeking and their exposure to the literature may become much more circumscribed in scope.

This is a serious problem, particularly if our efforts to teach end-users to search are limited to the mechanics and procedures of searching, if we rely on printed handouts and point-of-use assistance as our sole method of instruction, or if we offer only stand-alone workshops that focus on one system or database. I think we should be cautious not to let online searching instruction replace the entire content of our bibliographic instruction sessions, especially if the latter encompass such topics as structure of the literature, approaches to problem solving and information seeking, use of the bibliographically controlled record of knowledge, and communication patterns within the disciplines.

CONCLUSIONS

Now it seems to me that these problems that I have covered, however superficially, are the source of a whole host of problems that have been brought out by our other speakers. We do not really have a good understanding of what we do when we search, so we may be tempted to emphasize the mechanics of searching and simple linear search strategies. We do not know enough about the psychological relationships between users and systems to be able to customize our instruction to meet the needs of a varied clientele. We do not know enough about the knowledge-base with which our users work to design user-friendly software that overcomes the segmentation of information and at the same time functions at a level that users find both simple and satisfying. We are too tempted to rely upon simple handouts, particularly of vendor materials, and point-of-use instruction at the reference desk, as the survey report summarized yesterday indicated. We may be so eager to teach end-users to search that we ignore much of what we learned from our experience with bibliographic instruction programs over the years. Because of these fundamental problems that I have mentioned (and there are probably others as well), it may be hard for us

to decide on things like appropriate content, when to teach, where to teach, teaching method, or whom to teach. And since we have never really figured out how we search, and have never developed satisfactory methods for measuring our own searching performance, we have few firm ideas of how to evaluate our instructional efforts on any criteria other than user satisfaction or the mechanical aspects of searching.

But I want to assure you that I am no Luddite. I have never let any of these problems paralyze me. I am convinced that it is a disservice to our users not to share what we can, however inadequately we may do it. In many ways we are at a stage in teaching end-users to search that user education in general passed through some years ago. Some of us remember when library instruction concentrated primarily on the use of manual tools and library facilities. There was a great deal of effort expended on the mechanics of using card catalogs and printed indexes, on deciphering catalog cards and index citations. The transition to bibliographic instruction and more recently to information management education was a difficult one. It involved concentrating on our users' needs and information-seeking problems rather than on what we saw as deficiencies in the way they used the tools, and upon some of the fundamental problems associated with search strategies in manual systems. Today, much of what we do *best* in teaching end-users to search has to do with the mechanics and procedures of searching. If we are to get beyond that, a concerted effort will be required from the bibliographic instruction community to help overcome some of the fundamental problems that face us. We need to decide what the characteristics of really good user-friendly software are and communicate those to the designers of the systems. We need to try a variety of instructional approaches for different groups and try to decide what works best for whom. We need to come up with some good ways of helping students learn how to select terminology, develop flexible search strategies, and analyze their information needs.

As some of these problems are solved, or at least dealt with, we will probably see the solutions designed into software, making the systems truly user-friendly. It is not too farfetched to believe that we will see software relatively soon that overcomes some of the difficulties users have with controlled vocabulary--software that automatically maps to all appropriate subject headings and text words.[10] A little further along, we may see software that helps the user organize terminology and concepts in such a way that the system can perform Boolean searches for the user, developing its own strategy along the way. Such expert systems could go a long way toward solving the "black box" problem if properly designed.

In the meantime, I for one will continue to try to grapple with some of these underlying problems, teaching end-users to search as the opportunity arises, as well as I am able. I look on each occasion as an opportunity to learn more about the ways our users go about information-seeking and how we might help them along the way. I encourage you to do so as well.

NOTES

1.   John Kenneth Galbraith, *The New Industrial State*, 2d ed. (London: Andre Deutsch, 1972).

2.   Arnold Pacey, *The Culture of Technology* (Cambridge, MA: MIT Press, 1984).

3.   A short overview of the mechanical world view can be found in Jeremy Rifkin, *Entropy: A New World View* (New York: Viking, 1980).

4.   Frederick W. Lancaster, *Evaluation of On-Line Searching in MEDLARS (AIM-TWX) by Biomedical Practitioners* (Urbana, IL: Graduate School of Library Science, University of Illinois, Occasional Papers no. 101, 1972; Bethesda, MD: ERIC Document Reproduction Service, ED 062 989, n.d.).

5.   A non-technical discussion of current thought on human problem solving, how it differs from computer information processing, and new attempts at computer modeling can be found in William F. Allman, "Mindworks," *Science 86* 7, no. 4 (May 1986): 22-31.

6.   Carol H. Fenichel, "The Process of Searching Online Bibliographic Databases: A Review of Research," *Library Research* 2, no. 2 (Summer 1980-1981): 107-127.

7.   Sherry Turkle, "Computers as Rorschach," in *Inter/Media: Interpersonal Communication in a Media World*, ed. G. Gumpert and P. Cathcart. (New York: Oxford University Press, 1982); and Sherry Turkle, *The Second Self* (New York: Simon and Schuster, 1984).

8.   Leigh Estabrook, "The Human Dimension of the Catalog: Concepts and Constraints in Information Seeking," *Library Resources and Technical Services* 27 (January/March 1983): 68-75.

9.   Carol H. Fenichel, "The Process of Searching Online Bibliographic Databases."

10.   Some progress has been made in this area. See, for example, the description of the CITE system in Tamas E. Doszkocs, "Cite NLM: Natural-Language Searching in an Online Catalog," *Information Technology and Libraries* 4 (December 1983): 364-380. Since the article was written, the software has been extended for use in searching MEDLINE as well.

End-User Searching for the

Undergraduate Business Student:

A Course-Integrated Approach

Sharon Mader and Betsy Park

INTRODUCTION

The first part of this presentation will cover the background and development of the end-user search service at the Memphis State University Library, and how bibliographic instruction fits into that service. In the second part, my colleague Betsy Park will describe our bibliographic instruction program for end-users in the Business Communication classes.

In an article from *Omni* magazine of several years ago--one of those early "Eureka! It's online!" articles--the author professed his conversion to a new way of life in this way:

> On-line databases can make the same kind of difference in your life that your first calculator did. It's the difference between struggling to get information and having it, between guessing and knowing. For many of us, access to databases may be the best thing that our computers can give us.[1]

Since we are all involved in bibliographic instruction, we are all familiar with people "struggling to get information" and guessing, rather than knowing. I'd like to talk about the kind of instruction we might devise for people wanting to access the new user-friendly end-user systems.

There have been a number of studies on user interaction with online systems, but by and large these concerned specialized groups of users (such as engineers) using sophisticated systems. Since the user-friendly simplified search systems such

Mader is Information Retrieval Librarian, and Park is Reference Librarian, Memphis State University Library, Memphis, TN.

as BRS/After Dark are so new, not many studies have been reported as yet. We have to look first at *how* end-users search, and then we can be more specific about *what* instruction is needed.

We need to get our vis-à-vis end-users clear in our minds. There still seems to be a debate going on in some quarters about whether end-users can search, and whether they will return to search after you have spent time teaching them. We have just returned from a conference where a panel on end-user searching generated a heated debate on the librarian as "high priest" versus the "unwashed masses"; as trained searchers, of course, we can run rings around the end-user when it comes to doing a "good" search.

We are not competing with the end-users, however, and we are not training them to be like us. Instead, we need to look at what their purposes are in doing a search themselves. What do they expect to get? How often will they need to search? What learning will be retained? Should instruction be designed in progressive modules of increasing sophistication? What expectations do they have of the system?

END-USER PILOT STUDY

We did a pilot study in the spring of 1984 to explore the feasibility of introducing an end-user service in the library. We investigated faculty and graduate students' search performance on an end-user system, and also their attitudes toward such a system. A stratified random sample of faculty and graduate students performed a search on BRS/After Dark. Afterwards, half the subjects attended an instruction session, and then all subjects performed a second search.

The variables examined for effect of search performances were 1) research experience (faculty or graduate student), 2) instruction, and 3) amount of practice time. Multivariate analysis of variance indicated a significant difference only for the effect of time, for example, subjects did better on their second search session than they did on their first. Surprise!

Search performance was measured by counting 1) the number of commands used, 2) the number of Boolean combinations used, 3) the number of typographical and spelling errors, and 4) the number of non-typographical errors, such as errors of logic or duplicate commands. Also noted were the percentage of searchers using search modification and advanced techniques (such as nesting, truncation, and command stacking), as well as those who had system trouble.

AN END-USER SERVICE IN THE LIBRARY

Based on the positive results of our pilot study, we were able to establish an end-user service, called U-SEARCH, which complements our intermediary online service.

We feel very strongly that it is important to make end-user searching available in the library. Indeed, the survey of the participants in our study revealed that 44 percent would prefer to use the service in the library, as opposed to home (27 percent), or office (25 percent).

I'd like to briefly describe the service, because our end-user instruction is part of this service package. One of the handouts you have is the U-SEARCH Information Sheet (Appendix 1), which explains the hours, costs, and other details.

The service is available every evening (except Friday and Saturday), and on Saturday afternoons. U-SEARCH was initially designed to be self-service, because we didn't have any funds for extra staff. At the present time, the search sessions are monitored by a student assistant, who logs the patron onto the system, keeps track of the length of the search, changes the paper in the printer, and collects payment. We have now hired a library assistant, who will be responsible for the day-to-day operation of the service. In addition, this person will be trained to assist users during their search.

Since we must operate on a cost-recovery basis, users are charged a flat rate of $1.25 per five-minute blocks of online time. (This simplifies matters for the student assistant and makes it easy to tell patrons how much a search will cost.) This figure was based on the average cost of all the BRS/After Dark databases. The $15 an hour amount also corresponds to what the majority of participants in our study said they would be willing to pay. However, in face of rising database charges, we will soon be re-assessing our fee structure.

During our first year of service, beginning in March 1985, 300 searches were performed. The average cost per search was $5.35, with an average search lasting approximately 20 minutes. The user profile looks like this: faculty, 7.7 percent; graduate students, 67.3 percent; undergraduate students 23.7 percent; and outside users, 1.3 percent. Of the users who completed our post-search evaluation, 97 percent said they would use the service again.

END-USER INSTRUCTIONAL OPTIONS

One of our premises was to make the service available without restrictions to anyone (university or non-university), who wanted to use it, with or without instruction. But, equally, we saw teaching end-users as an important component, as well as a new adventure.

Consequently, we offer several instructional options as part of the service. On an individual basis, we provide professional consultation, and a computer-assisted instructional tutorial. For groups, we give classroom instruction, both single sessions and course-integrated sessions, which are part of an assignment. Also planned, but not yet provided, are seminars and workshops for various groups of users.

Professional Consultation

We strongly recommend that users avail themselves of consultation with a U-SEARCH librarian, even if they have participated in a class session. Of the users who filled out post-search evaluation forms, 15 percent had not consulted a librarian. Some of these were repeat users; others had attended a class session or worked through the tutorial, and apparently didn't feel a need for consultation.

The professional consultation has elements common to both the classroom presentation and to the intermediary search interview. On the one hand, you have to keep the consultation simple and avoid jargon; on the other hand, you have to convey certain pieces of information that remain transparent during an intermediary search interview because you know you are going to do the search. Since the end-users themselves will be making the final decisions on search strategy and system interaction, you are acting as a true consultant, preparing them to move through the steps themselves. The consultation takes about half an hour, depending on whether the user has attended a class presentation, and on user background and experience. At the end of the consultation an appointment is made for the search. The basic points covered during the consultation are as follows:

1. Service parameters
2. Topic definition
3. Database selection
4. Search strategy
5. Search system input
6. Printing results
7. Alternative strategies

Service Parameters

Service parameters are carefully explained so that users know what to expect: hours of service, costs, results (e.g., you get a printout, worldwide literature is covered, not just what is owned by our library), role of the student assistant, and instructional options (professional help available during the day, tutorial). At this point, we may advise the user that an intermediary or manual search would be more appropriate.

For the statement of the topic, search worksheet 1, "Concept Development," is used to identify concepts and keywords and to design the search strategy (Appendix 2).

Search worksheet 2, "System Input," is then used to translate the intellectual scheme from the first worksheet into what will actually be entered in response to system prompts. Databases to be used are listed here also (Appendix 3).

CLASSROOM INSTRUCTION

We feel that classroom instruction for end-users fits right into our existing program of bibliographic instruction for the following reasons:

1. We have always presented online databases, along with print information resources, in instruction sessions for graduate students, according to the information needs and information-seeking patterns of that discipline. Most of these were research methods or dissertation preparation classes. We now include end-user instruction or at least a description of the end-user service in the course-related presentations we do, both graduate and undergraduate.
2. Teaching online searching is complementary to teaching students or faculty how to use the online catalog.
3. Teaching online searching is teaching a method of thinking. The search strategy can be seen as representing the steps in the research process and can be used as a means of introducing students to this concept.

Critical thinking is an important element in teaching online searching. A recent article in the *Chronicle of Higher Education* about the new emphasis on critical thinking in college curricula made me realize how online searching fits perfectly into this scheme. "Faculty members teach students how to generate questions from hypotheses and how to break complex ideas and problems into small parts--skills that are the signs of a successful student."[2] This is, of course, what we have been doing all along, and now our efforts have a new justification and a new incentive for collaboration with the teaching faculty.

This recent approach to incorporating critical thinking into higher education has been dubbed "thinking across the curriculum"; why not "searching across the curriculum?" Let's emphasize (again) the problem solving skills inherent in what we are teaching.

In considering the format of the instruction, one conclusion that might be drawn from our study and other studies is that the type of instruction has an effect; hands-on experience appears to be critical. Garman and Pask, in their study of business students at Purdue, state that their participants "emphatically felt that they learned far more from the actual hands-on experience than from the demonstration and lecture."[3] The demonstration and lecture--two of our well-used methods.

End-users in our study found the system relatively easy to use; this is supported by the findings of other studies, such as Janke, Friend, and Trezbiatowski.[4] But users, in our study and other studies, said that instruction was necessary or very helpful, especially for the first-time user. This instruction would involve more than just the mechanics of the system. Linda Friend at Penn State noted that students had trouble with Boolean logic and breaking a topic down into its component concepts. I'm sure we can all identify with this, since students have the same kinds of problems with print sources.

The MARS Direct Patron Access to Computer-Based Reference Systems Committee has developed instructional objectives for library users and online systems.[5] These objectives cover four general areas:

1. Understanding the system
2. Planning the search strategy
3. Operating the system
4. Interpreting the search results

We cover these four areas--at a beginning level. When we first began teaching end-users, we tried to pack everything we knew about searching into one hour so that users would be ready to face the system. Now we have greatly simplified our approach. We realize that end-users need different levels of instruction. Since it appears that end-users do not have much difficulty dealing with the mechanics of the terminal or the search system, we concentrate our efforts on an understanding of the structure of the databases and on search strategy. We have two courses at present in which doing an online search is part of an assignment: Microcomputer Applications for Educators (graduate) and Business Communications (undergraduate).

BUSINESS COMMUNICATIONS AS A MODEL

Why Business Communications? Actually, it doesn't have to be Business Communications. We offer Business Communications here as a model for teaching online skills in any course, particularly a core course. For your own purposes, choose a course that will be a showcase, such as a required, upper-division, undergraduate course or a beginning graduate course. After you have worked with this course and developed a base of trained users, you can build upon basic skills by expanding to more specialized courses. Strike while the iron is hot! Be on the lookout for those courses that want to include new technologies in their content.

Business Communications, for example, is ripe in this respect. Pick up any business or computer magazine these days and there is usually an article on the "wonderful world of online." As microcomputers and automated workstations become common, and as the value of online information becomes recognized by decision-makers, new graduates will be expected to be aware of online services and how to use them. We just presented a paper at the Association for Business Communication's annual meeting in Mobile. The theme was communications and new technology, and the way we are using our new technology was news to the business school faculty that attended.

The basic rationale for including online searching in the business communications course, from a business school instructor's perspective, is that 1) it's a good way to introduce computer literacy, since searching does not require a knowledge of programming; 2) online resources are often virtually unknown to undergraduates; these skills are applicable and transferable to other academic courseworks; and 3) knowledge of online information resources provides good career preparation. The basic goal of the course unit is to introduce the undergraduate business student to online information services and their potential for both academic and business information needs.

We definitely have made undergraduates more aware of online information. Only 4 percent of those who use our intermediary service are undergraduates, in contrast to almost one-fourth of our end-users. As an aside, our end-user service in general has attracted those who have never done any searches or perhaps never been in the library.

Two recent articles I found on teaching online searching to business students are particularly interesting because they were written by business school faculty.[6] The objectives and content are similar to what we do, with the major difference being that they have done this all by themselves. They never refer to the library, except as a repository, nor have they consulted with a trained searcher or instruction librarian. They mention as a disadvantage the time and money involved in getting online training, since neither one of them knew anything about online searching before this.

How much better (and easier) it would have been for them if they would collaborate with librarians. End-users will be end-users--wherever they are. They are searching outside the library. It's important that we let them know how a partnership could benefit them.

In the literature, the value of business communication courses to the business curriculum has been documented by numerous studies, and this could probably be said of core courses in other disciplines. This value can be greatly enhanced by incorporating online searching into the curriculum. Betsy Park will now talk more about how this can be done.

BUSINESS COMMUNICATIONS AT MEMPHIS STATE UNIVERSITY

During this conference we have heard others emphasize the growing interest in and utilization of end-user searching in college and university libraries. Our knowledge of and research on training end-users is still, however, at a relatively primitive stage. There are few articles in the literature detailing the introduction of end-user searching and its relationship to the existing bibliographic instruction program. Sharon Mader has already told you about the end-user service, U-SEARCH, at Memphis State University. We have offered this service since March 1985, and continue to experiment with a variety of instructional methods. We have been particularly successful in introducing an end-user component in an undergraduate business communications class.

Background

In the Fogelman College of Business and Economics at Memphis State University, there are approximately 4,000 undergraduate students. The business communications class, part of the core curriculum, is a required course normally taken during the student's junior or senior year. Each semester there are usually eighteen sections of the class offered, with approximately 450 students enrolled. The class syllabus covers all areas of business communications. The course description reads: "Communication theory applied to solving business problems. Presentation of oral and written case solutions; emphasis on letters, memorandums, and reports. Attention given to job search strategy, research and writing." Thus it is a crowded class, both in the number of students taking the class and the amount of information covered. The students themselves are fairly traditional undergraduate students with a variety of levels of motivation and sophistication. Many have visited the library rarely.

For the past several years, we have come to the business communications class to give a lecture on the use of library resources for one of the writing assignments--the writing of a formal business report. The instruction sessions stressed a conceptual approach to the research process, helping students to identify their research needs and analyze the need to formulate a research strategy. For the business report, students must analyze a situation and make appropriate recommendations based on a literature review (secondary data) and a survey (primary data). Our lecture concentrated on locating secondary data; we had always mentioned the library's online information retrieval service and when the U-SEARCH service became established, we began suggesting it as an alternative.

Two of the business communications instructors became enchanted with "electronic information retrieval" or the online search process. Although they had never actually performed a search themselves, they both had had searches done in the library. These instructors recognized the importance of information access in the business world and felt their students would be better prepared for "life after MSU" if they had experience with the new technology. They also hoped that the introduction of online information sources might even stimulate those students so aptly called "the chairs" to more active classroom participation.

After meeting with these instructors, we decided to change the traditional bibliographic instruction lecture for their classes to one that concentrated on end-user searching. They added a sentence to the course description that stated "online bibliographic searching would be introduced." We knew we could count on the enthusiasm and cooperation of these instructors to help ensure that the students would perceive the assignment as an important class requirement. We began working with these classes during the summer of 1985 and have continued each semester with six to eight sessions per semester. Thus far, we have talked to approximately 500 business communications students. As with everything else we do, the design of the online search module has changed every semester. What I shall describe is the most recent version.

The Assignment

Because the syllabus for the business communications course was already overcrowded, we were forced to incorporate the module on online searching without making any drastic change in the course. Time is of critical importance--we are limited to one class period ranging from one hour to one and a half hours. The topics for the reports vary with the class; the students have a choice of three or four topics, usually concerned with current events, rather than being strictly business-oriented. Students have written on the passage of a seat belt law in Tennessee and the placement of vending machines in resident halls, among other topics. One of the instructors has his students write on whether or not to incorporate an online search module into the business communications curriculum--allowing the students to write about what they are doing in class. Students work in groups of three to five to gather the background information; the reports are written individually.

Goals and Objectives

The goal of the online module is to introduce undergraduate business students to online information services, and to their potential for both academic and business information needs. The aim is for students to see this as a useful resource both for their undergraduate/graduate years and for the world of business beyond the university.

There are five objectives of the module for the students: 1) to be aware of new trends in information technology that will affect information access in business; 2) to understand the different kinds of databases and the variety of information available; 3) to be able to translate an information request into a form acceptable to an online system; 4) to demonstrate a knowledge of the mechanics of online searching; and 5) to demystify the online search process.

Outline of the Module

The online search module includes:

1. Advance organizers
   a. Background readings placed in the reserve book room
   b. Pre-search assignment in the library
2. Class presentation by librarians on online searching
3. Computer-assisted instruction tutorial
4. Online search by student groups
5. Writing of business report

Advance Organizers

Since it is virtually impossible to accomplish all that we want in the limited time available, we have had the instructors introduce the idea of online searching by showing students copies of searches they have done and talking about some of the uses of an online search. In addition, we have placed several readings in the reserve room,[7] which will provide the students with background information.

Students are also required to complete an assignment, which involves coming to the library and locating citations using the library's computer catalog, *Readers' Guide, Business Periodicals Index*, and the *Wall Street Journal Index*. Students note how they used these sources, keywords used, and at least five useful citations. These exercises ensure that the majority of students 1) know where the library is located; 2) have had experience using a computer to locate information; and 3) have used print indexes to locate journal articles.

Classroom Presentation

The advance organizers allow us to concentrate on the search process during the classroom sessions. We begin by referring to the preliminary searches the students have done on their topic and compare the manual and the online research process, noting the advantages and disadvantages of each. Prior preparation is more important for an online search because students must pay for the online search according to the time spent online. We stress that the research process is similar, whether using an online or a print source.

Using the search worksheet (Appendix 2), we walk through the steps in developing a search strategy. We work through several examples, writing out the research questions, underlining key terms, identifying concepts, and expanding and combining concepts. This process is similar to the traditional research process and to the critical thinking exercises Sharon has mentioned.

After discussing the intellectual plan, we look at a second search worksheet (Appendix 3), which details how the strategy will be input into the system. The mechanics of the input process often confuse students. We suggest that students input one word or phrase at a time and then combine. We have also found it useful to instruct students to use only one type of Boolean connector in a search statement--this alleviates the problems of the hierarchical nature of connectors. We discuss how students will interact with the system, print their results, and locate the relevant information sources in the library. Following the presentation, the librarians and the instructor circulate the room to help students complete their search worksheets. Sometimes this can be accomplished during the classroom sessions; more often students need to talk with a librarian at a later time. Students do have to complete the worksheets for the assignment; they are not required to talk with a librarian.

In class, students have also received handouts that cover definitions of online terminology, database descriptions, U-SEARCH policies, and a short bibliography. Students can use these handouts in writing their reports.

Computer-Assisted Instruction Tutorial

We have developed a computer-assisted instruction tutorial, which students use to help them with the mechanics of the online search. It allows them to gain some familiarity with the BRS/After Dark system before they go online and also with the Apple IIe computer we use for the service (most business students are more familiar with an IBM computer). The tutorial allows students to perform a simulated "canned" search on After Dark--interacting with the search menu by typing in a specified search. We are still in the process of developing the CAI, and are modifying what we have. We hope to expand it to cover search strategy and more complicated search procedures.

Online Search Session

The online search session has been handled in a number of different ways, primarily because we are dealing with a large number of students each semester. The search is performed by students working in groups (3 to 5 per group). One student is designated "the typist" and the others help coach. One option is to include the search as part of a second class session--for which we use BRKTHRU (the daytime counterpart of After Dark). A second option is to have the students use the U-SEARCH service on their own time. At the beginning, we were present during the students' search, but found it difficult not to "butt in." During the spring semester, we had the students use the service just like other patrons, consulting with a librarian during the day if they wanted additional help and performing the search with only a student assistant present. This seemed to work fairly well and shall probably be continued. We now have a library assistant to work with the U-SEARCH service, so some help will be available during the search.

At Memphis State University, students must pay for their searches. Most searches on U-SEARCH run under 20 minutes or $5, and the average cost per student (working in groups) has been about $1.

EVALUATION

We have not yet identified an appropriate evaluation tool, and as yet have not attempted to formally evaluate the program. The module is introductory and quite basic. It does not attempt to train students to be self-sufficient searchers, but to introduce the undergraduate student to a new technology, and to help this student locate information for a written assignment. It is important that the student begin to see the online service as another information resource in the library. As we train more students and they become more sophisticated in the use of online bibliographic resources, they will need more extensive training.

We have noticed informally that several of these students have returned to use U-SEARCH for a paper in another class the following term, and have recommended that their friends use the service. A few think it is the only way to find information in the library.

Another factor indicating success is that the instructors' enthusiasm and commitment has not abated. They have become, if anything, more interested in the project each semester, and have begun presenting the project at their professional meetings.

We have looked at some of the papers written as a result of the online module--particulary those recommending that online searching be incorporated in the regular business curriculum. Sometimes the students can say it as well as we can. To quote from one paper: "Just as the business department has incorporated the use of the computer facilities into the statistics courses, the business department should incorporate the use of U-SEARCH into the office administration course." Another student mentions the benefits of online searching--to help combat the "as soon as possible syndrome." Another states, "If students were more educated on the 'how's' and the 'why's' of the retrieval system, then it is certain that they will make use of the computer in the future. Where there is no education of something--there is no knowledge of it."

CONCLUSIONS AND RECOMMENDATIONS

1. End-user searching should be integrated into the traditional BI program. Look at the classes you teach, and identify those that could benefit from a module.
2. End-user searching can be introduced without dramatically changing the syllabus of a particular course--you may be forced to do some juggling, but it is possible to introduce the module even with strict limitations on time.
3. Keep it simple. Make a checklist of what the student has to know if it is a first-time contact. Remember you will be training a core of students who will eventually be as familiar with online sources as with other sources (often they have no knowledge of either when you start).
4. Develop worksheets--they are very helpful in planning search strategy.
5. Use a variety of instructional tools and methods. In our module we have a short lecture, small group discussions, CAI practice, hands-on search, and the actual writing of the report.
6. Be aware of the role of expectations--both yours and the students. Often these are not in sync.
7. Choose a class in which you will get optimal results--one that can be used as a showcase for others.

8.   Enjoy teaching end-users--it is a learning experience for all involved.

NOTES

1.   Owen Davies, "Databases Madness," *Omni* 6 (November 1983): 26,28.

2.   Liz McMillen, "Many Professors Now Start at the Beginning by Teaching Their Students How to Think," *Chronicle of Higher Education* 32 (5 March 1986): 23-25.

3.   Nancy J. Garman and Judith M. Pask. "End-User Searching in Business and Management," in *National Online Meeting Preceedings--1985*, 161-165. Compiled by Martha E. Williams and Thomas H. Hogan. (Medford, NH: Learned Information, 1985).

4.   Richard V. Janke, "Online After Six: End User Searching Comes of Age," *Online* 8 (November 1984): 15-22; Linda Friend, "Independence at the Terminal: Training Student End Users to Do Online Literature Searching," *Journal of Academic Librarianship* 11 (July 1985): 136-141; Elaine Trzebiatow-ski, "End User Study on BRS/After Dark," *RQ* 23 (Summer 1984): 446-450.

5.   Dennis Hamilton, "Library Users and Online Systems: Suggested Objectives for Library Instruction," *RQ* 25 (Winter 1985): 195-197.

6.   Keith Adler, *Online Secondary Research in the Advertising Research Class: A Friendly Introduction to Computing.* (Bethesda, MD: ERIC Document Reproduction Service, ED 243 148); Craig E. Daniel, "Online Information Retrieval: An Underutilized Educational Tool," *Information Services & Use* 4 (August 1984): 229-243.

7.   The reserve list includes: Ryan R. Hoover, *Executive's Guide to Online Information Services.* (White Plains, NY: Knowledge Industry Publications, 1984), 1-8, 19-20; Dean Howitt and Marvin I. Weinberger, *Inc. Magazine's Databasics: Your Guide to Online Business Information.* (New York: Garland Publishing, 1984), 3-12; Bryan Pfaffenberger, *The College Student's Personal Computer Handbook.* (Berkeley: Sybex, 1984), 105-123; Daniel Seligman, "Life Will Be Different When We're All Online," *Fortune* 111 (4 February 1985): 68-72.

MSU LIBRARIES
U-SEARCH SERVICE

Have you ever had tremendous problems locating information? Have you spent hours searching for references on the benefits of sports for the handicapped, or other topics? You may want to try using one of MSU Libraries' computerized search services: the Information Retrieval Service (IRS) or U-SEARCH.

U-SEARCH is a new library service which allows you to perform your own online search using BRS/After Dark. This service offers you access to approximately 50 databases to find information on a variety of topics, including Business and Finance, Education, Social Sciences, and Science and Medicine.

U-SEARCH differs from the Libraries' Information Retrieval Service in that you do the search yourself rather than having a librarian intermediary perform the search for you. While online you will have the opportunity to print out the results of your search and leave the session with search results in-hand. You now have a choice of using a printed index, having a professional librarian perform the search, or doing one on your own. Although professional consultation is not available while you perform the search, you may talk with a professional searcher either before or after you do your search.

U-SEARCH will allow you to gather a list of references on your topic, often with an abstract. A few full text databases are also available.

WHERE:	Information Retrieval Office Reference Department- Room 103 MSU Libraries
WHEN:	The service is available evenings and weekends during these hours:

> Sunday   7:00pm- 9:30pm
> Monday   6:30pm - 9:30pm
> Tuesday   6:30pm - 9:30pm
> Wednesday   6:30pm - 9:30pm
> Thursday   6:30pm - 9:30pm
> Saturday   12:30pm - 5:00pm

Appointments are recommended, but not necessary.

COST:	MSU faculty, staff, and students
	    $1.25 per five minute intervals of online time
	Patrons outside the University
	    $2.00 per five minute intervals of online time

Payment must be made upon completion of the search. <u>NO CASH;</u> checks or preauthorized transfer vouchers <u>only</u>.

HELP:	Search worksheets and manuals available in the IRS office. A computer-assisted tutorial introduces you to After Dark & lets you do a practice search.

To make an appointment for a search or for consultation, call 454-2208 and ask for a U-SEARCH librarian

Sharon Mader and Betsy Park: Addendum

SEARCH WORKSHEET 1 : CONCEPT DEVELOPMENT

Plan your search strategy by following these steps:

STEP 1. Describe your search topic in one or more sentences.
(Be as clear and concise as possible. Think in terms of facets
of the question, rather than the expected answer. For example,
"What is the most effective method to teach mathematics to elementary
school students who are bilingual?" is a better question than "What
do I do with children who don't speak English?")

Search topic:_____

_____

_____

STEP 2. Break the topic down into concepts.
(It will help to underline the key ideas, as in the example above.
Then write each separate concept in the boxes below. The number of
concepts you use will depend on your topic. Concepts may be single
words or word phrases.)

CONCEPT A	CONCEPT B	CONCEPT C

STEP 3. List alternative ways of expressing the concepts.
(You can expand or narrow your topic by listing under each concept
synonyms, word variants, or related terms.)

STEP 4. Reconstitute your topic by combining the concepts.
(Terms within each box can be linked with OR - meaning any of these.
Terms across boxes can be linked with AND - meaning all must be present.
OR broadens the search, while AND narrows the search.)

Sharon Mader and Betsy Park: Addendum

MEMPHIS STATE UNIVERSITY   LIBRARIES

U-SEARCH SERVICE

SEARCH WORKSHEET 2:   SEARCH INPUT

CATEGORY: _____ ;   DATABASE(S): _____ _____ _____

CATEGORY: _____ ;   DATABASE(S): _____ _____ _____

SEARCH TERMS: (enter as many or as few as you want)

S1 -->

S2 -->

S3 ->

S4 ->

S5 ->

S6 ->

S7 ->

S8 ->

S9 ->

S10 ->

(PRINT sequence on back)

Sharon Mader and Betsy Park: Addendum

U-SEARCH SERVICE

PRINT SEQUENCE:

SYSTEM PROMPT	EXPLANATION
XX -> Enter a search question to print from (e.g. 1 or 2 ,etc)	Enter only the number of the search set you want to have printed.
XX -> Enter S for short print form, M for medium print form, or hit enter for long print form.	See print format samples in notebook to choose the format you want.
XX -> Enter document number(s) to be printed. Use a hyphen for sequential documents (x-x), commas for non-sequential documents (x,x,x) or enter individual number (x). Type all to print all documents or hit enter to print first document.	Consider typing all; there is an automatic stop after each screen.

Sharon Mader and Betsy Park: Addendum

Memphis State University Libraries

Database Descriptions

ABI/INFORM (1971-present)

ABI/INFORM database is designed to meet the information needs of executives and covers all phases of business management and administration. Stresses general decision sciences information which is applicable to many types of businesses and industries. Specific product and industry information is included but does not receive primary emphasis. Indexes approximately 550 publications.

BUSINESS SOFTWARE DATABASE (Current Information)

Business Software Database contains descriptions of over 3,500 software packages which have business applications for use with micro and minicomputers. Records in the Business Software Database include a description of the package; the name, address, and phone number of the manufacturer; and the price and number of packages sold. Records also include information on the availability of the software, machine capability, the program language, description of the documentation, and availabilty of cutomer service assistance and other services from the manufacturer.

ERIC (1966-present)

ERIC is the complete database on educational materials from the Educational Resources Information Center. It consists of two main files: Resources in Education, which is concerned with identifying the most significant and timely education research reports and projects; and Current Index to Journals in Education, an index of more than 700 periodicals of interest to every segment of the education profession.

MAGAZINE INDEX (1959 to March 1970, 1973 to present)

Magazine Index is the first online database to offer truly broad coverage of more than 435 general interest magazines. Provides extensive coverage of current affairs, the performing arts, business, sports, recreation and travel, consumer product evaluations, science and technology, leisure time activities, and other areas.

NATIONAL NEWSPAPER INDEX 1979-present (1982-present for the Los Angeles Times and the Washington Post)

The National Newspaper Index provides front-to-back indexing of the Christian Science Monitor, the New York Times, and the Wall Street Journal. All articles, news reports, editorials, letters to the editor, obituaries, product evaluations, biographical pieces, poetry, recipes, columns, cartoons and illustrations, and reviews are included. The only items not included are weather charts, stock market tables, crossword puzzles, and horoscopes.

PAIS (1976-present)

PAIS (Public Affairs Information Service) contains references to information in all fields of social science including political science, banking, public administration, international relations, economics, law, public policy, social welfare, sociology, education and social anthropology. Over 800 English language journals and 6,000 non-serial publications are indexed each year. PAIS provides comprehensive coverage on all issues of public policy regarding social, economic or political problems including information on such areas as accounting; municipal, state and federal administration; consumer attitudes; multinational corporations; and Congressional hearings.

Sharon Mader and Betsy Park: Addendum

Online Information Services
Definitions

ABSTRACT

A concise summary of an article, book or other
publication

BIBLIOGRAPHIC

A record or citation containing essential information
about a publication. It usually consists of the title
of the publication, the author(s) or editor(s), the
name of the page numbers (if an article) and the date
of publication.

DATABASE

A collection of related information in machine-readable
form usually stored on magnetic disk or tape. Databases
may be numeric, textual or both. A database can be
reference (including bibliographic), which tells you
where to get the complete information, or source, which
contains the complete information. Source databases
may be numeric or full-text.

END USERS

Persons using online services who will actually be
using the resulting information.

INFORMATION PROVIDER

The organization that provides the information or
databases offered by an online service. Also called
database supplier or database publisher. Information
providers may be publishers, wire services, stock
exchanges or government agencies.

ONLINE

The condition when a person (through a terminal) or a
computer is communicating with another computer via
telephone, leased line, cable or other communications
channels.

ONLINE SERVICES

A computerized information, transaction or communication
service with which a user can communicate by telephone,
cable, satellite or other communications channels.
Also called interactive service.

OFFLINE

The state when a computer is not communicating with
other computers but is doing all of its work locally
on its own processors.

RECORD

A unit of information received from an online service.
A record may be a few lines to several pages long,
depending on the type of information represented. A
bibliographic record is usually only a few lines long,
while a full-text record may be quite long. Numeric
records may be of any size.

Sharon Mader and Betsy Park: Addendum

Memphis State University Libraries

┌─── The Future of Computerized Research ───┐

As the amount of business information grows, on-line data
bases will enlarge and multiply, and they probably will become the primary source of business information. The high
speed and extreme accuracy of electronic searching, the huge
volume of materials that can be stored and readily accessed
for searching and printing and the phenomenal expansion in
the number and size of on-line data bases over the past decade will make computerized information retrieval systems
the primary research tools of the future. No existing system of manual indexing or numbering can be effective for
information storage and retrieval as computerized systems,
especially those with free-text search capability. As
smaller, more efficient, higher capacity hardware such as the
random access memory chip is used, future search costs will
be reduced and the use of on-line data bases will become increasingly common in small and large CPA firms, businesses,
schools and homes.

From "Computerized Research:
An Advanced Tool" By Andrew
P. Gale, Journal of Account-
ancy, 153 (1982): 84.

Glossbrenner, Alfred. The Complete Handbook of Personal Computer Communications.
    New York: St. Martin's Press, 1983. (REF QA 76.5 G535 1983)

Hoover, Ryan E. Executive's Guide to Online Information Services. White Plains,
    NY: Knowledge Industry Publications, Inc. 1984.

Howitt, Doran, and Marvin I.Weinberger. Inc. Magazine's Databasics: Your Guide
    to Online Business Information. New York: Garland Publishing, Inc., 1984
    (REF HF 5548.2 H67 1984)

Lisanti, Suzana. "The Online Search." BYTE 9 (December, 1984): 215-230.

McGuire, Peter J. "The On-line Literature Search in the Business Writing Class."
    ABCA Bulletin 44 (June 1981): 30-32.

Pfaffenberger, Bryan. The College Student's Personal Computer Handbook. Berkley,
    California: SYBEX, 1984. (REF LB 2395 P43x) Kept in IRS office.

*See also materials on Reserve (4th Floor) for Dr. Valesky, EDAS 7440, Microcompu-
ter Applications.

Sharon Mader and Betsy Park: Addendum

INTRODUCTION TO ONLINE SEARCHING

--- ONLINE CATALOG

--- IRS/U-SEARCH

--- MANUAL SEARCH IN A PRINT INDEX

Sharon Mader and Betsy Park: Addendum

STEPS IN DEVELOPING
THE SEARCH STRATEGY

1. STATING THE PROBLEM

2. IDENTIFYING CONCEPTS

3. CHOOSING TERMS

4. COMBINING TERMS

Sharon Mader and Betsy Park: Addendum

SEARCH WORKSHEET 1

CONCEPT DEVELOPMENT

STEP 1:   DESCRIBE YOUR SEARCH TOPIC

IN ONE SENTENCE OR IN THE FORM

OF A QUESTION.

SEARCH TOPIC: _____

_____

Sharon Mader and Betsy Park: Addendum

SEARCH WORKSHEET 1

CONCEPT DEVELOPMENT

STEP 2:   BREAK THE TOPIC DOWN INTO CONCEPTS.

CONCEPT A	CONCEPT B	CONCEPT C

Sharon Mader and Betsy Park: Addendum

SEARCH WORKSHEET 1

CONCEPT DEVELOPMENT

STEP 3: WORKING WITHIN EACH BOX,

LIST ALTERNATIVE WAYS OF

EXPRESSING THE CONCEPTS.

CONCEPT A	CONCEPT B	CONCEPT C

Sharon Mader and Betsy Park: Addendum

SEARCH WORKSHEET I

CONCEPT DEVELOPMENT

STEP 4: RECONSTITUTE YOUR TOPIC BY
COMBINING THE CONCEPTS

OR   AND
WITHIN BOXES   ACROSS BOXES
ANY OF THESE   ALL OF THESE
BROADENS   NARROWS

Sharon Mader and Betsy Park: Addendum

THE ONLINE TUTORIAL

LESSON SECTION MENU

1. LEARN MORE ABOUT ONLINE SEARCHING

2. LEARN MORE ABOUT BRS/AFTER DARK

3. DO A PRACTICE SEARCH ON BRS/AFTER DARK

4. DO ALL THREE SECTIONS

5. QUIT FOR NOW

Sharon Mader and Betsy Park: Addendum

LESSON 1, SECTION 3

DOING A PRACTICE SEARCH ON BRS/AFTER DARK

OBJECTIVES FOR PRACTICE SEARCH ON BRS/AFTER DARK

AFTER COMPLETING THIS SECTION YOU WILL BE ABLE TO DO
THE FOLLOWING:

1. KNOW HOW TO USE A "MENU" SYSTEM.

2. UNDERSTAND AND USE THE BASIC BRS/AFTER DARK COMMANDS

3. PERFORM A SIMPLE SEARCH ON BRS/AFTER DARK

Sharon Mader and Betsy Park: Addendum

SYLLABUS

BUSINESS COMMUNICATION
OFAD 3510

Dr. Binford H. Peeples, Professor
Department of Office Administration
Fogelman College of Business and Economics
Memphis State University
Memphis, TN 38152
Telephone: (901) 454-2886

COURSE DESCRIPTION: Communication theory applied to solving business problems. Presentation of oral and written case solutions: emphasis on letters, memorandums, and reports. Attention given to job search strategy, research, and writing. online bibliographical search introduced.

ACTIVITIES:

1. Lectures and explanations
2. Class discussions
3. Presentation of illustrative material with the overhead and opaque projectors and with chalkboard
4. Audio-Visual Presentations (including a video program on the MSU's U-Search facility in the Brister Library)
5. Guest Speakers (including Reference Librarians who will give instructions for using online bibliographical search)
6. In-Class writing exercises
7. Out-of-Class writing exercises
8. Tutorial program for the U-Search Bibliographical Service and "hands-on" experience in obtaining secondary information for use in recommendation report.
9. Discussion and evaluation of written communication
10. Short oral presentations by students (outside readings and library work)
11. Discussion and evaluation by students and teacher of written and oral business messages
12. Chapter quizzes, Unit test, In-Class Writing Exercises, Out-of-Class Writing Assignments, and a comprehensive final exam

OUTLINE OF COURSE CONTENT

1. Introduction to communication theory
2. The Communication Process (Listening, Speaking, Writing, Reading, and Thinking)
3. Nonverbal Messages
4. Interpersonal Communication
5. Writing for Readability
6. Writing for Persuasion
7. Special Kinds of Business Writing (Letters, Memorandums, and Reports)
8. Functional Business Reports
9. Collecting Secondary Information (Print Indexes and Electronic Databases)
10. Collecting Primary Information (Developing and Using Questionnaires)
11. Organizing and Interpreting Information
12. Oral Reporting
13. Job Search Strategy
14. Communication Technology and Systems
15. Cost Effective Communication

Sharon Mader and Betsy Park: Addendum

SYLLABUS

BUSINESS COMMUNICATION   Page 2
OFAD 3510

GRADING:

Chapter Quizzes	Short-answer questions (True/False and Multiple Choice) related to reading assignments, a class routine that may be expected at any time without previous announcement
Unit Tests	These assignments will cover major topics covered in the text and parallel readings, the date, subject and nature of these tests will be announced as far in advance as possible
Examination	A comprehensive short-answer examination based on the major topics covered in the text and parallel reading assignments

> *Scores on Chapter Quizzes, Unit Tests, and Examinations will be constitute fifty percent of the final grade in this course.

In-Class Writing Writing Assignments	A class routine that may be expected at any time without previous announcement--always related to assigned reading, make-up work is not planned
Out-of-Class Writing Assignments	A class routine planned to provide opportunities for demonstrating communication skills, all work should be in the best possible form--this usually means typewritten (A copy should be retained for your files. Adherence to the schedule is urgent. Credit will be awarded for work turned in <u>on time</u> and <u>as directed</u>, make-up work is not planned

> *Evaluations of the writing assignments will constitute fifty percent of the final grade in this course.

Note:	A tutorial program on the use of the U-Search procedure is available at the Learning Media Center in the Brister Library. The Online Bibliographical Research Service can be scheduled through the Reference Department in the Brister Library.

---

*The following grading scale will be used: A = 95 to 100, B = 85 to 94, C = 75 to 84, D = 65 to 74, F = 0 to 64

Sharon Mader and Betsy Park: Addendum

End-User Searching and

Bibliographic Instruction

Nancy Taylor and Sara Penhale

Earlham College is a liberal arts college with a long-standing and extensive bibliographic instruction program. Three years ago, we began incorporating end-user searching into our program. Teaching students to do their own online searching seemed more appropriate to our goal of providing students with a variety of information retrieval skills than did our prior practice of conducting searches for them. We hoped that online searching skills would be additional preparation for our students' future information needs in graduate schools or in jobs.

We began our end-user training program on a small scale. It presently consists of course-integrated instruction in which we provide online training for the research needs of students in specific courses. Generally the instruction consists of a one-hour lecture in which an explanation of databases, search strategy formulation, Boolean operators, and the mechanics of conducting the search is provided, followed by individual appointments during which we review the student's search strategy and assist as necessary during the search.

BEGINNING AN END-USER SEARCHING PROGRAM

Several characteristics of the classes initially selected for the end-user training program added to the ease with which our program was developed. First, by using a course-integrated approach we ensured that the students would be motivated by actual research needs at the time of their training. Secondly, the courses we selected were upper-level offerings in the biology and psychology departments, populated by students skilled with the print tools

Taylor is Reference Librarian, Lilly Library, Earlham College, Richmond, IN and Penhale is Science Librarian, Wildman Science Library, Earlham College, Richmond, IN.

Nancy Taylor and Sara Penhale   57

of their disciplines and with library research strategies. These two departments have incorporated an extensive program of bibliographic instruction into their courses, beginning with the introductory courses, and continuing in advanced-level courses. In addition, the specific subject areas, evolutionary biology, clinical medicine, and experimental psychology, have journal literature, which is accessible in one or two well-organized databases, such as *Biological Abstracts*, *Index Medicus*, or *Psychological Abstracts*.

By initially limiting end-user training to a few classes, we hoped to become familiar with the benefits and problems associated with searching by undergraduates before developing a larger scale educational program. The outcome of our early experience was, therefore, thoroughly monitored. Using a variety of evaluation procedures gave us a clearer picture of the significance of an online search than we would have gained had we only asked the students to rate the relevancy of the citations retrieved and their overall satisfaction at the time of their searches. For instance, asking students to evaluate their searches *after* they used the information to complete their assignments resulted in a more accurate assessment of the effectiveness of the searches. Questioning them about other search techniques or sources they used helped to reveal the role of online searching in the overall information retrieval process.

Comparing the bibliographies of completed assignments with search printouts was a means of documenting the use made of the online searches. Finally, the faculty who evaluated the students' completed work were another source of information about the effectiveness of information retrieval.

RESULTS OF INITIAL END-USER SEARCHING PROJECTS

We have reached a number of conclusions regarding the ability of undergraduate students to conduct searches, and the role of online searching in providing information for research assignments.

Online Searching for Term Papers

Students working on traditional term paper assignments can benefit from online searching. Students who used an online search to supply citations for a term paper on evolution reported that many of the citations retrieved were relevant to their research needs, and that they did in fact read many of the relevant articles. The bibliographies of their completed term papers included articles listed on their online printouts. The on-line search was only a part of the research process, however. Students reported spending an average of four hours prior to the search, primarily in the process of defining their term paper topics, and an average of nine hours afterward locating articles and then using their bibliographies, or doing citation searches on articles located through the online search. In the bibliographies of the students' term papers, only one-third of the citations were on the online printout. The average number of citations in the student bibliographies was fifteen, a small number relative to the amount of literature available on the topics. This is evidence that undergraduate research needs are not comprehensive in scope, and an indication that an end-user search can be useful even if it does not provide as extensive a list of relevant sources as a search by a professional librarian might. Not all the students in this biology class conducted online searches. In the process of using print tools to define their paper topics, these individuals were able to locate sufficient resources for their papers.

Online Searching for Class Discussion

In another course, online searching allowed the students to participate in an innovative class assignment that would have been impractical or impossible if library research had been limited to manual techniques. Students in a comparative psychology class participated in weekly discussions on course topics, such as learning or social behavior. Throughout the term, each student was asked to report on a specific type of animal. Each student's contribution to the discussion was a brief report on some of the recent articles on their animal groups. Manual searching would have been tedious, if not impossible, for some of the students, whose assigned groups of animals were not extensively studied.

Because the students searched an average of six times over a ten-week term, the effect of practice on improving search capability became apparent to us. Time for each search decreased significantly over the course of the project and the students were increasingly satisfied with their searches, and more confident of their online skills.

Online Searching for Abstracts of Articles not Available in the Library

A third end-user project involved a biology class in which the students are required to write papers evaluating the effectiveness of commonly prescribed treatments for medical problems, basing their evaluations on the primary medical literature. Because Earlham's medical journal collection is limited, the list of medical problems has been tailored to match the information available in our journals. Relying on interlibrary loan had not been considered as a solution to this limitation, because the students must write two papers in a ten-week term and do not have time to wait for borrowed material.

Online searching of *Index Medicus* in the course allowed the students to quickly identify relevant literature, and obtain abstracts for articles not in our library. The faculty members judged that papers citing a combination of online abstracts and available articles were equivalent in quality to papers citing complete articles. In other words, the online abstracts provided information that was sufficient to supplement the information obtained by reading available articles. This allowed students to select topics of interest to them in spite of limited holdings in Earlham's library on that topic.

The appropriate search strategy for this assignment was straightforward--a combination of the disease concept and the treatment concept. We designed an end-user instruction program that included a variety of specialized search techniques for increasing the specificity of the searches. For instance, the students were taught how to determine the *MESH* subject headings for the medical problem and the treatment, to use descriptors to identify clinical research articles, to limit the citations to journals in the Earlham library, or to limit the citations to those with online abstracts. The librarian learned that beginning searchers can be taught to use a number of special techniques at the same time as they are learning basic online skills.

END-USER SEARCHING WITHIN A BIBLIOGRAPHIC INSTRUCTION PROGRAM

Reflecting on these experiences, we have begun to assess the place of end-user searching in an overall bibliographic instruction program. When end-user instruction was initiated at Earlham, we envisioned it as an optional "final step" in providing students with the research skills needed in the present and future information environment. Since that time, we have come to believe that students *must* be taught to use both print and electronic reference sources.

Such training is necessary because reference sources exist now, and will probably continue to exist, in a mixture of formats. For instance, at the present time, electronic databases predominately represent "economically important" information. Information from fields not tied to business or industry, such as the humanities, are underrepresented in the online environment. While more databases in other areas are being created, it is

unlikely that some types of sources, such as the great variety of bibliographies in literature or sources that present an alternate point of view, such as the *Left Index*, will soon be computerized. Conversely, some databases only exist in electronic form or may not be locally available and thus can be accessed only through online searching.

In addition to reaching the conclusion that training for computerized searching is necessary, we have also come to believe that the needed education will not fundamentally differ from that already provided in bibliographic instruction programs. Librarians should continue to follow the principles that have made their instruction effective in the past, and librarians should expect that students' attitudes and behavior with regard to library use will remain the same.

Course-Integrated Instruction

Many have observed that end-users who participate in training programs do not necessarily conduct online searches later. One explanation may be that they did not have a pressing information need at the time they were trained. In the past, instruction programs for the use of print tools have been successful when presented in response to an information need. When faculty demand use of the literature, students are motivated to learn how to find it. There is no reason to conclude that the motivation to conduct online searches will be based on different criteria; thus instruction should be provided within the context of an academic course requiring the use of library literature.

Providing instruction at the time of need will also mean that students will immediately put into practice what they have just learned; an important factor given the amount of detail involved in using online systems. In addition, the instruction can be tailored to the specific course in a variety of ways; for instance, restricting instruction to the specific databases needed for that course assignment.

Graduated Instruction

It is clear that with practice, students become more proficient as library researchers. Just as this is true with the use of print sources, so it has been shown to be true for online searching. Creating a sequential bibliographic instruction program will allow the librarian to introduce more sophisticated techniques or reference sources after the students have mastered the rudimentary skills of literature searching.

Staging instruction for electronic searching could occur in many ways; use of field limiters could be taught after simple use of search terms, or instruction in full-text searching could follow bibliographic searching. In addition, there may be several ways by which electronic searching can be integrated into the overall graduated library research curriculum. We have found that students can be effectively taught online searching after they have a good foundation in using the print version of a database, and we have also successfully taught students to use both the print and online versions of a database simultaneously.

Librarians should be cautious, however, with regard to the level of online search expertise they expect from their students. Because we hold ourselves, as search intermediaries, to high standards, we have a tendency to expect the same from our end-users. We should not conclude, however, that end-user searches are not useful if they don't conform to our expectations. We should remind ourselves that we usually assume that students' print searches are effective, even though it may be true that a trained librarian could locate the information more efficiently.

Concepts of Searching

A bibliographic instruction program that focuses on concepts of searching rather than on the mechanical details of using specific sources allows students to apply what they have learned to various types of searching. For instance, the processes of recognizing the different elements of a search topic, of considering how to narrow or broaden the topic, of choosing key words or subject headings to express the elements of the topic are as central to performing online searches as they are to using print sources. If these conceptual skills are developed, students will be able to move back and forth between print and electronic sources in the course of a literature search.

Just as students must learn which print reference sources are relevant to a given information need, selection of appropriate electronic databases should also be taught. While some user-friendly search systems provide a database selection option, the selection is based solely on number of "hits." The system does not make qualitative judgments about the type of information that will be provided. All information seekers must learn to make such assessments as they search for the best information for their needs.

Students' Information Needs

When questioned, our students said they would prefer to use a combination of print and online searching when using the library. The most effective technique may depend on how much information is needed, how complex the search strategy must be, or the particular stage of the research process. Teaching students to search both print and online will enable them to make their own informed judgment concerning the best path to the needed literature.

Students' Attitudes and Behavior

In general, student response to end-user searching has been very positive. They find it quick and productive, and many find it fun. These students are comfortable using computerized information systems because they use computers in other aspects of their education.

On the other hand, we see students encountering the same problems with the use of end-user searching as with the use of print reference tools. Some procrastinate and delay their online searches until shortly before the assignment is due--too late to effectively utilize most of the information located. Other students do not like to read documentation prepared by the vendor or by the instruction librarians. There are individuals who avoid using a computer, while others want to use electronic tools to the exclusion of print.

CONCLUSION

Up to this point, most college instructional programs for end-user searching have been constrained by the financial limitations of the currently available online systems, which charge by the amount of time a database is being used. With emerging technologies, such as CD-ROM or other flat-fee pricing structures, the time the user spends searching will no longer be limited by cost. This will allow students to consult the databases just as they would use other freely accessible print reference tools. With this accessibility, students can browse freely, explore the contents of the database, and become comfortable with searching techniques. Searching skills will improve considerably with practice, along with students' searching success and satisfaction. Then instruction in electronic searching can be integrated more fully with traditional bibliographic instruction.

Nancy Taylor
Lilly Library
Earlham College

COMPARATIVE PSYCHOLOGY

September 1984

Annual Review of Psychology. v. 1, 1950- . On wall shelves.
    Each volume contains 13 to 18 reviews of the literature in various topical
areas of psychology. Since 1958 the plan has been to present certain important
topics (e.g., Developmental Psychology, Psychotherapy) each year; others will
appear every second, third, or fourth year and a few irregularly -- all depending on their importance and amount of new literature. The bibliographic essay
on each subject covered is by an authority in the field. They cover the important literature and emphasize interpretation and evaluation. There are
author and subject indexes in each volume as well as 5-year cumulative indexes
of chapter titles. The library has volume 1 to date. Exceptionally useful for
keeping up with recent developments in particular areas of psychology.

Biology
    and psychology, 1–2
    history of, 24–25
Birds
    imprinting among
        and early experience
        studies, 119–23,
        135–36
Birth order
    and intelligence, 630
Birth trauma

133. Lindholm, B. W. 1962. Critical periods
    and the effects of early shock on later
    emotional behavior in the white rat. *J.
    Comp. Physiol. Psychol.* 55:597–99
134. Lorenz, K. 1935. Der Kumpen in der
    Umwelt des Vögels. *J. Ornithol.* 83:
    137–214; 289–413. Translated by au-
    thor and republished as "The compan-
    ion in the bird's world." *Auk* (1937)
    54:245–73
135. Maltzman, I., Raskin, D. C. 1965.
    ...ial differences in the
    ...n conditioning and
    ...s. *J. Exp. Res. Pers.*

    958. Effects of early
    ...on adult behavior in
        Physiol. Psychol.

    ...rivation

Imprinting
Although Spalding and various other naturalistic observers noted that
precocial birds (i.e. those able to locomote at the time of hatching) will
follow the first moving object they see, it was Lorenz (134) who first called
this phenomenon "imprinting" (his own translation from the German word

Social Sciences Index. June 1974 to date. (formerly Social Sciences & Humanities
    Index, 1965 to March 1974, and International Index, 1907 to 1965). On index
    shelves.
    The Social Sciences Index is an author and subject index to more than 260
of the most important scholarly periodicals in the fields of anthropology, area
studies, economics, environmental science, psychology, public administration,
sociology and related subjects. Only 77 social science periodicals were covered
by its predecessor, the Social Sciences & Humanities Index. Book reviews are
listed at the back of each issue. Issued quarterly with annual cumulations.

Bird calls
    Development of responsiveness to suprathreshold acoustic
        stimulation in chickens. L. Gray and E. W. Rubel. bibl J
        Comp & Physiol Psychol 95:188-98 F '81
    Effects of domestication on production and perception of
        mallard maternal alarm calls: developmental lag in behav-
        ioral arousal. D. B. Miller and G. Gottlieb. bibl il J Comp
        & Physiol Psychol 95:205-19 Ap '81
Bird song
    Oh, for the song of a bird. Economist 275:100 Ap 25-My 1
        '81

Nancy Taylor and Sara Penhale: Addendum

<u>Psychological Abstracts</u>. 1927 to date. On index shelves.
        Published by the American Psychological Association, this is the leading
abstracting medium in the field. Coverage includes books, reviews and
discussion papers as well as articles and reports in over 700 domestic and
foreign journals. Though many languages are covered, abstracts are all in
English. Abstracts of research literature give briefly the problem, method,
subjects used and principal results and conclusions. There is an author and a
brief subject index in each issue, and an annual author and more detailed
subject index for each bound volume. The library has volume 14 (1940) to date.

Subject Index

Birds ⁶⁷
UF Fowl
B   Vertebrates
N   Blackbirds
    Budgerigars
    Canaries
    Chickens
    Doves
    Ducks
    Geese
    Penguins
    Pigeons
    Quails
    Robins
    Sea Gulls

Birds
transition from self feeding to central place foraging, wheatears,
    comment on article by G. H. Orians & N. E. Pearson, 11983
ultraseasonal reproduction costs, house sparrows, 12031
vegetation & ground & frugivorous foraging, American robins, 400
visual threat displays during agonistic encounter, parrots, 2780
vocalizations & dominance & other characteristics, blue vs Steller's vs
    hybrid jays, 7299
vocalizations & territoriality & courtship behavior, sharpbills, Costa
    Rica, 12060
voluntary regulation of lighting in Skinner boxes, domestic fowl, 346
wing fluttering, frequency of attacks, female cliff swallows, 360

Abstracts

12060. Stiles, F. Gary & Whitney, Bret. (U Costa Rica,
Escuela de Biología, San José) Notes on the behavior of the
Costa Rican Sharpbill (*Oxyruncus cristatus frater*). *Auk*,
1983(Jan), Vol 100(1), 117–125. —Male Costa Rican sharpbills
apparently form exploded leks of 3–4 birds, advertising their
territories by singing a high, thin, wiry, descending trill from
conspicuous perches high in the canopy of precipitous, mideleva-
tion rain forest. The bright vermilion crest of the males is erected
during intense aggressive interactions but not during singing.
Probable courtship is also described, along with a probable flight
display of unknown significance. Sharpbills employ varied
foraging tactics and take both fruit and animal prey. The
sharpbills' bill and foraging appear to represent a unique
specialization within the great tyrannine suboscine radiation of
the New World tropics and a striking convergence with the
family Icteridae in particular. (14 ref)

<u>Social Sciences Citation Index</u> (<u>SSCI</u>). 1973 to date. On index shelves.
        This is published in three main sections: Citation Index, Source Index
and Subject Index. The Citation Index lists a book or article and tells you
where that book or article has been cited. The Source Index is, in effect, an
alphabetical listing of virtually all current literature in the social sciences.
The Subject Index lists those same items by two keywords from the title: e.g.,
Negroes/Jobs or Women/Wages. For coverage before 1973 see <u>Science Citation</u>
<u>Index</u> (Science Ref/Z/7401/S3.65) which has included an increasing number of
psychological journals since 1963 and other social science journals since 1966.

Citation Index

GOTTLIEB G

Source Index

GOTTLIEB G

Nancy Taylor and Sara Penhale: Addendum

Searching BRS/After Dark

Turn on the terminal.
Turn on the modem.

Dial 8-9-634-5708

When you hear the high pitched sound, place the receiver in the modem.
Hit return twice, again if no response.

Information entered by the user is underlined. Always press the return key to enter a response.

```
TELENET
317 19A

TERMINAL=decw          Type in "decw", return.

@c 315 20b             Type "c 315 20b", return.

315 20B CONNECTED

ENTER BRS PASSWORD
████████████          Passwords will be available from the librarians
ENTER A-M-I-S PASSWORD    when you come to search.
████████████

*SIGN-ON   20.02.40                    09/20/84:


WELCOME TO BRS AFTER DARK

PLEASE TYPE IN SCREEN LINE LENGTH (20, 40, OR 80)   No need to respond for this
                                    terminal. Just press return!
PLEASE TYPE IN THE NUMBER OF LINES ON YOUR
SCREEN (20,21,22, ETC.)             Just press return again.

   CHECK MENU ITEM 6 FOR INFORMATION ON NEW
   AFTER DARK DATABASES AND SYSTEM ENHANCEMENTS.
   SIX NEW DATABASES HAVE BEEN ADDED TO THE SYSTEM
   SINCE JULY, 1984!!!!!!!!

TONIGHT'S MENU IS:

NUMBER          ITEM                              Read the menu and
   1            LOOKING FOR INFORMATION?...SEARCH SERVICE   choose the desired
   2            WANT TO HEAR THE LATEST?...NEWSLETTER SERVICE  action. To search the
   4            KEEP IN TOUCH!...ELECTRONIC MAIL SERVICE   database, select
   6            WHAT'S NEW?...NEW SYSTEM FEATURES          number 1.
   7            WANT TO CHANGE YOUR SECURITY PASSWORD?...
                SECURITY
```

Nancy Taylor and Sara Penhale: Addendum

```
TYPE IN MENU ITEM NUMBER THEN HIT ENTER KEY FOR DESIRED SELECTION
     1
```
Type "1", press return.

```
YOU ARE NOW CONNECTED TO THE BRS AFTER DARK SEARCH SERVICE.
THE FOLLOWING CATEGORIES OF DATABASES ARE AVAILABLE FOR
SEARCHING.
CATEGORY       DESCRIPTION

     1         SCIENCE AND MEDICINE DATABASES
     2         BUSINESS AND FINANCIAL DATABASES
     3         REFERENCE DATABASES
     4         EDUCATION DATABASES
     5         SOCIAL SCIENCE AND HUMANITIES DATABASES

TYPE IN CATEGORY NUMBER THEN HIT ENTER KEY FOR
CATEGORY OF DATABASES DESIRED.     5
```
Type "5", return

```
SOCIAL SCIENCE AND HUMANITIES DATABASES
*******************************************
DATABASE NAME                              LABEL

ABLEDATA - OF NARIC                        ABLE
FAMILY RESOURCES                           NCFR
MENTAL MEASUREMENTS YEARBOOK               MMYD
NATIONAL REHABILITATION INFORMATION        NRIC
  CENTER
PUBLIC AFFAIRS INFORMATION SERVICE         PAIS
PRE-PSYC                                   PREP
PYSCINFO                                   PSYC
RELIGION INDEX                             RELI
SOCIAL SCIENCE CITATION INDEX              SSCI
SOCIOLOGICAL ABSTRACTS                     SOCA

TYPE IN LABEL FOR DATABASE DESIRED:     PSYC
```
Type the label, psyc, return.

```
WOULD YOU LIKE INSTRUCTIONAL PROMPTS? PLEASE TYPE
YES OR NO:     yes
```
For new users the instructional prompts are helpful. Type yes, return.

```
WOULD YOU LIKE A DESCRIPTION OF THE DATABASE?   (YES OR NO)     no
```
Since you are familiar with Psychological Abstracts, do not ask for a description of it.

```
BRS/PSYC/1967 - SEP 1984
TYPE IN SEARCH TERM, OR ENTER COMMAND:
     M TO RETURN TO MASTER MENU,  D TO CHOOSE NEW DATABASE,
               OR O TO SIGN OFF.
S1 -->    cricket$
```
When prompted by the arrow, type in a search term. Note that the term has been truncated by the $ so that the computer will search for cricket, crickets, or any other endings.

set number
```
A1     99   DOCUMENTS FOUND  <——
TYPE IN SEARCH TERMS, OR ENTER COMMAND
     P TO PRINT DOCUMENTS FOUND, R TO REVIEW SEARCH QUESTIONS,
     M TO RETURN TO MASTER MENU, D TO CHOOSE NEW DATABASE,
  OR   O TO SIGN OFF.
S2 -->    sons$
```
After a pause, the computer will indicate how many citations relate to your search terms.

Continue searching.

set number
```
A2     529  DOCUMENTS FOUND
TYPE IN SEARCH TERMS, OR ENTER COMMAND
     P TO PRINT DOCUMENTS FOUND, R TO REVIEW SEARCH QUESTIONS,
     M TO RETURN TO MASTER MENU, D TO CHOOSE NEW DATABASE,
  OR   O TO SIGN OFF.
```

Nancy Taylor and Sara Penhale: Addendum

```
S4 -->     1 and 2
```

Combine terms by using their set numbers with the operators: and, or.

```
A4     14  DOCUMENTS FOUND
TYPE IN SEARCH TERMS, OR ENTER COMMAND
       P TO PRINT DOCUMENTS FOUND, R TO REVIEW SEARCH QUESTIONS,
       M TO RETURN TO MASTER MENU, D TO CHOOSE NEW DATABASE,
   OR   O TO SIGN OFF.

S6 -->     P
```

14 citations deal with crickets and songs.

Above we will print some of the citations to see if they are relevant.

```
ENTER A SEARCH QUESTION TO PRINT FROM (E.G. 1 OR 2, ETC.)   4
ENTER S FOR SHORT PRINT FORM,   M FOR MEDIUM PRINT FORM,
OR HIT ENTER FOR LONG PRINT FORM.     S
```

When you ask for the short form, the complete citation is printed.

```
ENTER DOCUMENT NUMBER(S) TO BE PRINTED.  USE
A HYPHEN FOR SEQUENTIAL DOCUMENTS (X-X),
COMMAS FOR NON-SEQUENTIAL DOCUMENTS (X,X,X),
OR ENTER INDIVIDUAL NUMBER (X).  TYPE ALL TO
PRINT ALL DOCUMENTS OR HIT ENTER TO PRINT FIRST
DOCUMENT.
       1-5
```

Ask to see a subset of the articles first to see if your search process has produced relevant articles.

```
 1
AU CAMPBELL-D-JAMES.  LOHER-WERNER.
TI A MICROCOMPUTER-BASED MODULATOR FOR SIMULATING INSECT SONGS AND THE
   RESPONSE OF CRICKETS TO AN ARTIFICIAL CALLING SONG.
SO BEHAVIOR RESEARCH METHODS & INSTRUMENTATION.
   1983 OCT VOL 15(5) 538-541.
 2
AU ELLIOTT-C-J.  KOCH-U-T.
TI SENSORY FEEDBACK STABILIZING RELIABLE STRIDULATION IN THE FIELD
   CRICKET GRYLLUS CAMPESTRIS L.
SO ANIMAL BEHAVIOUR.
   1983 AUG VOL 31(3) 887-901.
 3
AU LATIMER-W.  SCHATRAL-A.
TI THE ACOUSTIC BEHAVIOUR OF THE BUSHCRICKET TETTIGONIA CATANS: I.
   BEHAVIOURAL RESPONSES TO SOUND AND VIBRATION.
SO BEHAVIOURAL PROCESSES.
   1983 MAY VOL 8(2) 113-124.
 4
AU CADE-WILLIAM-H.
TI FIELD CRICKET SPACING, AND THE PHONOTAXIS OF CRICKETS AND PARASITOID
   FLIES TO CLUMPED AND ISOLATED CRICKET SONGS.
SO ZEITSCHRIFT FUR TIERPSYCHOLOGIE.
   1981 VOL 55(4) 365-375.
 5
AU LATIMER-WILLIAM.
TI THE ACOUSTIC BEHAVIOUR OF PLATYCLEIS ALBOPUNCTATA (GOEZE)
   (ORTHOPTERA, TETTIGONIIDA).
SO BEHAVIOUR.
   1981 VOL 76(3-4) 182-206.
END OF DOCUMENT.  HIT ENTER TO SEE NEXT DOCUMENT, OR
TYPE ANOTHER DOCUMENT NUMBER, OR
TYPE S TO CONTINUE SEARCHING, P TO PRINT DOCUMENTS FOUND,
R TO REVIEW SEARCH QUESTIONS, M TO RETURN TO MASTER
MENU, D TO CHOOSE NEW DATABASE, OR O TO SIGN OFF.
```

Nancy Taylor and Sara Penhale: Addendum

That was a very simple search, combining only two terms. Keep your search structure as simple as possible, but of course endless combinations are possible if needed for your search. Let's try a little more complex search.

```
TYPE IN LABEL FOR DATABASE DESIRED:    PSYC
```
Selected psyc again.

```
WOULD YOU LIKE INSTRUCTIONAL PROMPTS? PLEASE TYPE
YES OR NO: ---- no ----------------------------------------
```
Once you are comfortable with searching, prompts are not necessary.

```
WOULD YOU LIKE A DESCRIPTION OF THE DATABASE?  (YES OR NO)    no
```

```
BRS/PSYC/1967 - SEP 1984
TYPE IN SEARCH TERMS OR ENTER COMMAND
S1 -->     bird$ and (song$ or vocal$)
```
It is possible to save steps by entering several search terms with Boolean operators in one request.

```
A1     485  DOCUMENTS FOUND
TYPE IN SEARCH TERMS OR ENTER COMMAND
S2 -->     learning
```
This is a very large set, which can be further narrowed to answer a more specific question.

```
A2     58220  DOCUMENTS FOUND
TYPE IN SEARCH TERMS OR ENTER COMMAND
S5 -->     1 and 2
```

```
A5     74  DOCUMENTS FOUND
TYPE IN SEARCH TERMS OR ENTER COMMAND
S6 -->     geographic$
```

```
A6     1103  DOCUMENTS FOUND
TYPE IN SEARCH TERMS OR ENTER COMMAND
S7 -->     6 and 5
```

```
A7     3  DOCUMENTS FOUND
TYPE IN SEARCH TERMS OR ENTER COMMAND
S8 -->     geographic$ or area$ or location
```
Further narrowing results in a very small set, so try using other descriptors.

```
A8     23704  DOCUMENTS FOUND
TYPE IN SEARCH TERMS OR ENTER COMMAND
S9 -->     8 and 5
```

```
A9     4  DOCUMENTS FOUND
TYPE IN SEARCH TERMS OR ENTER COMMAND
S10 -->    p;9;s;1-4
```
Still small, but print them to see if they are relevant. Commands for printing can be entered one at a time as in the previous search, or strung together.

```
 1
AU CUNNINGHAM-MICHAEL-A.  BAKER-MYRON-C.
TI VOCAL LEARNING IN WHITE-CROWNED SPARROWS: SENSITIVE PHASE AND SONG
   DIALECTS.
SO BEHAVIORAL ECOLOGY & SOCIOBIOLOGY.
   1983 VOL 13(4) 259-269.
```

Nancy Taylor and Sara Penhale: Addendum

```
   2
AU KING-ANDREW-P.  WEST-MEREDITH-J.
TI EPIGENESIS OF COWBIRD SONG: A JOINT ENDEAVOUR OF MALES AND FEMALES.
SO NATURE.
   1983 OCT VOL 305(5936) 704-706.
   3
AU KING-ANDREW-P.
   WEST-MEREDITH-J.
   EASTZER-DAVID-H.
TI SONG STRUCTURE AND SONG DEVELOPMENT AS POTENTIAL CONTRIBUTORS TO
   REPRODUCTIVE ISOLATION IN COWBIRDS (MOLOTHRUS ATER).
SO JOURNAL OF COMPARATIVE & PHYSIOLOGICAL PSYCHOLOGY.
   1980 DEC VOL 94(6) 1028-1039.
   4
AU CATCHPOLE-CLIVE-K.
TI INTERSPECIFIC TERRITORIALISM AND COMPETITION IN ACROCEPHALUS
   WARBLERS AS REVEALED BY PLAYBACK EXPERIMENTS IN AREAS OF SYMPATRY
   AND ALLOPATRY.
SO ANIMAL BEHAVIOUR.
   1978 NOV VOL 26(4) 1072-1080.
END OF DOCUMENTS IN LIST.
TYPE ANOTHER DOCUMENT NUMBER, OR
ENTER COMMAND    s            Return to searching

TYPE IN SEARCH TERMS OR ENTER COMMAND
S10 -->    sparrow$           A search revision from the citations received.


A10    156  DOCUMENTS FOUND
TYPE IN SEARCH TERMS OR ENTER COMMAND
S11 -->    10 and 5


A11    14  DOCUMENTS FOUND
TYPE IN SEARCH TERMS OR ENTER COMMAND
S12 -->    11 not 9        Use not to eliminate overlap with the set already printed.


A12    13  DOCUMENTS FOUND
TYPE IN SEARCH TERMS OR ENTER COMMAND
S13 -->    p;12;s;1-4

   1
AU MARLER-PETER.
   PETERS-SUSAN.
TI LONG-TERM STORAGE OF LEARNED BIRDSONGS PRIOR TO PRODUCTION.
SO ANIMAL BEHAVIOUR.
   1982 MAY VOL 30(2) 479-482.
   2
AU DOOLING-ROBERT-J.
   SEARCY-MARGARET-H.
TI A COMPARISON OF AUDITORY EVOKED POTENTIALS IN TWO SPECIES OF SPARROW.
SO PHYSIOLOGICAL PSYCHOLOGY.
   1981 SEP VOL 9(3) 293-298.
```

Nancy Taylor and Sara Penhale: Addendum

```
    3
AU MARLER-PETER.
   PETERS-SUSAN-S.
TI SPARROWS LEARN ADULT SONG AND MORE FROM MEMORY.
SO SCIENCE.
   1981 AUG VOL 213(4509) 780-782.
    4
AU DOOLING-ROBERT.
   SEARCY-MARGARET.
TI EARLY-PERCEPTUAL--SELECTIVITY-IN-THE-SWAMP-SPARROW.
SO DEVELOPMENTAL PSYCHOBIOLOGY.
   1980 SEP VOL 13(5) 499-506.
END OF DOCUMENT.  HIT ENTER TO SEE NEXT DOCUMENT, OR
TYPE ANOTHER DOCUMENT NUMBER, OR
ENTER COMMAND    o        Enter O, for off, to end the search.

*CONNECT TIME   0:06:23 HH:MM:SS     0.106 DEC HRS     SESSION  283*

*SIGN-OFF  22.27.46               09/20/84:
315 20B DISCONNECTED 00 00
```

Nancy Taylor and Sara Penhale: Addendum

```
                     Online Searching
              Search Strategy Practice Questions


        Design online seach strategies for the following questions.
Note all the search terms you would use and how you would combine
them using and, or, and not.  If the resulting set is too small, how
would you broaden the search?  If it is too large, how would you
narrow the search?  You may use both thesaurus and free text terms.

1.  How do birds learn their songs?  Is there a difference between
    learning of territorial and mobbing vocal behavior?




2.  What impact do critical periods have in social development, and
    specifically, in imprinting?




3.  What is the influence of mothering on the development of maternal
    behavior?
```

Nancy Taylor and Sara Penhale: Addendum

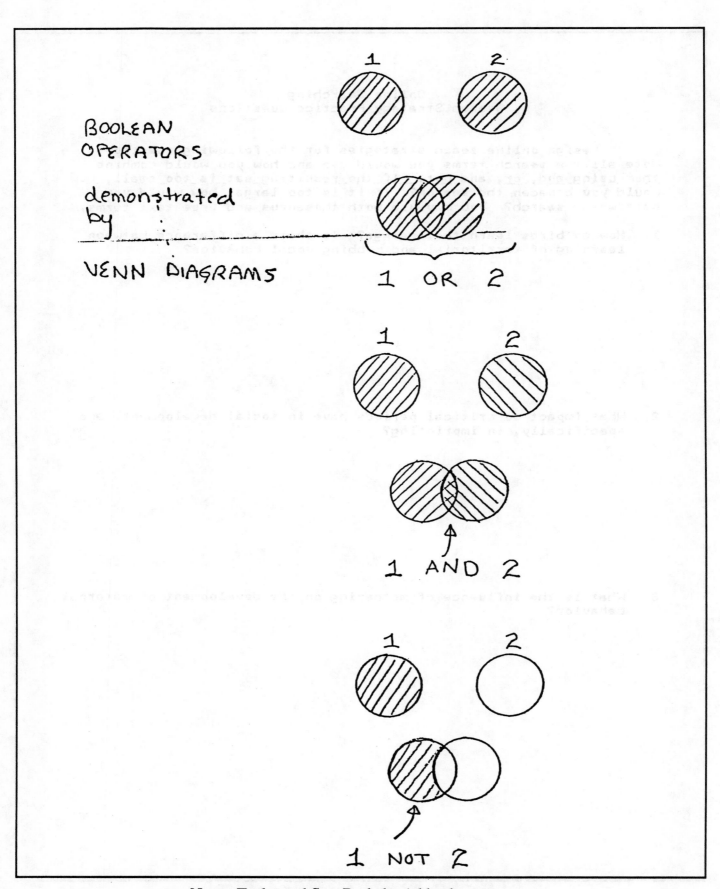

BOOLEAN
OPERATORS

demonstrated
by :

VENN DIAGRAMS

1 OR 2

1 AND 2

1 NOT 2

Nancy Taylor and Sara Penhale: Addendum

7.0 RESPONSIBLE PATIENTHOOD PAPER

Sara Penhale
Wildman Science Library
Earlham College

Refer to the DIAGNOSED CONDITIONS AND PRESCRIBED TREATMENTS table and imagine that you, your friend or a member of your family had one of the conditions listed and was advised to treat it with the prescription shown. As a responsible patient, investigate the nature of the condition and the proven effectiveness of the prescribed treatment. Begin by reviewing LIBRARY RESOURCES ON MEDICAL TOPICS (pages 47-57) and then proceed to research the topic in the Wildman Science Library. The immediate objective of your investigation will be a two-three page paper followed by a five minute oral report. The goal of the assignment is to become familiar with sources and methods of using the library to enhance personal awareness and improve health.

Prepare a two-three page type-written, double-spaced essay which covers:
1. a description of the condition and its symptoms
2. the etiology (cause) of the condition
3. the prognosis (outcome) of the condition
4. the effectiveness of the prescribed treatment, its side effects and contraindications (conditions under which it should be not used). Present the evidence.
5. a comparison of the relative effectiveness of alternate treatments. Present the evidence

OPTIONAL: you may wish to include the mode of action of the treatments, if they are known and if the explanations are not beyond the scope of this course.

Organize your paper in whatever arrangement seems logical and effective. Cite at least five sources, two of which must be primary sources (articles in which the results of an empirical investigation are reported for the first time). In the text of your paper, cite the sources of your information and list the sources you cited in a "Literature Cited" section at the end of the paper. Refer to FORMAT FOR CITING REFERENCES (page 43) for specific directions and be sure to cite only the pages actually referred to in books and other longer works, e.g. Woolpy, J. 1985. Human Biology. Earlham College Biology Department, Richmond, IN., page 40. Not, Woolpy, J. 1985. Human Biology. Earlham College Biology Department, Richmond, IN., pages 1-87.

As you work on your paper, refer to the RESPONSIBLE PATIENTHOOD PAPER CHECKLIST for reminders of correct format. The checklist will be used when your paper is graded.

Nancy Taylor and Sara Penhale: Addendum

7.2 DIAGNOSED CONDITIONS AND PRESCRIBED TREATMENTS

*Indicates trade name - consult drug indexes for ingredients

flu prevention - vaccination
manic-depression - lithium
ulcers - bland diet
hypertension - salt-free diet
colds - antihistamines
jock itch - tolnaftate
alcoholism - disulfiram
migraine headache - biofeedback
strep throat - antibiotics
depression - long distance
    running
skin problems - hydrocortisone
asthma - Vanceril*
diverticulitus - high fiber diet
menopausal hot flashes - estrogen
strep throat - penicillin
sun sensitivity - PABA
cystitis - cranberry juice
traveler's diarrhea - Pepto-Bismol*
hyperactivity - additive-free diet
acne - benzoyl peroxide
bad breath - Scope*
genital herpes - acyclovir
bed-wetting - imipramine
Crohn's disease - prednisone
athletic injury pain - cortisone
schizophrenia - chlorpromazine
acne - Accutane* (synthetic
    Vitamin A)
overweight - starch blockers
knee problems - arthroscopic
    surgery
new-born infant - breast-feeding
gonorrhea - penicillin
periodontal disease - oral surgery
hypoglycemia - high protein diet
angina - Inderal*
depression - electroconvulsive
    shock
pre-menstrual syndrome -
    anti-prostaglandins
swimmer's ear (otitis
    externa) - ear drops
lung cancer risk - low-tar
    cigarettes
preventing organ transplant
    rejection - cyclosporins

menstrual cramps - Midol*
tardive dyskinesia - propanolol
psoriasis - anthralin
chronic tension - tranquilizers
infertility -- fertilization in
    vitro (test tube babies)
chemotherapy nausea - nabilone
Parkinson's disease - L-dopa
breast cancer - radical mastectomy
amenorrhea in female runners -
    weight gain
vaginal yeast infections - nystatin
insomnia - sleeping pills
colds - vitamin C
irritable bowel syndrome -
    psychotherapy and diet change
opiate addiction - clonidine
bromidosis pedalis (smelly feet) -
    sandals
disc disease - chymopapain
coughs - dextramethorpan
chronic pain - oral morphine
cervical cancer - laser surgery
kidney failure - dialysis
heart disease - chelation therapy
angina - calcium channel blockers
heart attack - thrombolytic therapy
rabies - vaccination
prostatitus - antibiotics
precocious puberty - luteinizing
    hormone releasing hormone
poison ivy - Calamine lotion
anorexia nervosa - psychological
    counseling
schizophrenia - neuroleptics
sore throat - Listerine*
neonatal jaundice - phototherapy
obesity - jejunoileal bypass
respiratory distress syndrome -
    dexamethasone
epilepsy - valproic acid
unwanted pregnancy - "morning
    after pill"
multiple sclerosis - ACTH
    (adrenocorticotropic hormone)
hemorrhoids - Tronolane*
cervical cancer - laser surgery

Nancy Taylor and Sara Penhale: Addendum

```
              SAMPLE SEARCH FOR  "Depression -- Electroconvulsive Shock"


TYPE IN SEARCH TERMS

S1 -->depressive disorder and electroconvulsive therapy
A1      378  DOCUMENTS FOUND


S2 -->1 and (clinical trials or evaluation studies)
A2      27  DOCUMENTS FOUND

S3 -->2 and author.ab.
A3      20  DOCUMENTS FOUND



"PRINTING" THE DOCUMENTS IN SHORT FORM
         1
AN 86024673.  8601.
AU Horne-R-L.  Pettinati-H-M.  Sugerman-A-A.  Varga-E.
TI Comparing bilateral to unilateral electroconvulsive therapy in a
   randomized study with EEG monitoring.
SO Arch-Gen-Psychiatry. 1985 Nov. 42(11). P 1087-92.


         2
AN 86016694.  8601.
AU Kiloh-L-G.
TI The trials of ECT.
SO Psychiatr-Dev. 1985 Summer. 3(2). P 205-18.


         3
AN 85295621.  8500.
AU Varghese-F-T.  Singh-B-S.
TI Electroconvulsive therapy in 1985--a review.
SO Med-J-Aust. 1985 Sep 2. 143(5). P 192-6. (REVIEW).


         4
AN 85253539.  8500.
AU Gregory-S.  Shawcross-C-R.  Gill-D.
TI The Nottingham ECT Study.  A double-blind comparison of bilateral,
   unilateral and simulated ECT in depressive illness.
SO Br-J-Psychiatry. 1985 May. 146. P 520-4.


         5
AN 85200136.  8500.
AU Hyrman-V.  Palmer-L-H.  Cernik-J.  Jetelina-J.
TI ECT: the search for the perfect stimulus.
SO Biol-Psychiatry. 1985 Jun. 20(6). P 634-45.
```

Nancy Taylor and Sara Penhale: Addendum

"PRINTING" THE DOCUMENTS IN LONG FORM

```
        4
AN 85253539.  8500.
AU Gregory-S.  Shawcross-C-R.  Gill-D.
IN Mapperley Hospital, Nottingham.
TI The Nottingham ECT Study.  A double-blind comparison of bilateral,
   unilateral and simulated ECT in depressive illness.
SO Br-J-Psychiatry. 1985 May. 146. P 520-4.
LG EN.
AB Sixty nine patients took part in a double-blind study to investigate
   the efficacy of bilateral, unilateral, and simulated ECT in the
   treatment of depressive illness.  The findings suggest that both
   bilateral and unilateral ECT are highly effective treatments for
   depression and are significantly superior to simulated ECT.  There
   was also evidence that patients receiving bilateral ECT recovered
   more rapidly than those receiving unilateral ECT and required
   significantly fewer treatments.  The relevance of these findings to
   clinical practice is discussed.  Author.
MJ DEPRESSIVE-DISORDER: th.  ELECTROCONVULSIVE-THERAPY.
MN CLINICAL-TRIALS.  COMPARATIVE-STUDY.  DOUBLE-BLIND-METHOD.  HUMAN.
   PSYCHIATRIC-STATUS-RATING-SCALES.  SUPPORT-NON-U-S-GOVT.
SB M.
YR 85.
IS 0007-1250.
ZN Z1.542.363.300.
IM 8511.
ED 850827.
```

clinical trials
evaluation studies
drug evaluation

author.ab.

a.sb.

85.yr.

N-Engl-J-Med

Changing Perspectives Evolving from Diverse

End-User Applications

Sharon A. Balius

The University of Michigan Engineering College has been actively introducing computer integrated education into all programs for the past three years. The Computer Assisted Engineering Network (CAEN) deployed numerous large laboratories for students, each containing a wide variety of state-of-the-art computer equipment. In addition, each faculty member selected equipment for their offices. Thirty computers from CAEN were also merged into the Engineering-Transportation Library's study area when the first shipment arrived. Another one hundred have been added between our two facilities. The engineering libraries were therefore provided a prime setting for future database end-user searching. The computer has been well-established as an alternate source of information in the educational process. Engineering disciplines by their nature develop analytical techniques and they understand the potential applications of Boolean logic. Impetus for early end-user experiments was further provided by the knowledge that these computers would be networked to the Computing Center's mainframe and that the Michigan Terminal System would allow access to external systems via a 9600 baud telecommunications pad.

Our end-user experiments and programs were developed by staff in a variety of ways whenever an opportunity seemed suitable to involve students or faculty. Library research is not included in the engineering curriculum for lower undergraduates at our university so the students involved were juniors, seniors, or graduate students. Examples of end-user projects ranged from integrating the process into a semester-long information course taught by the head of the engineering libraries

Balius is Reference Librarian, Engineering Libraries, University of Michigan, Ann Arbor, MI.

for the last several years, to class lectures or seminars at faculty request. Also included were an informal semester-long experiment, presentations to faculty on the College's Library Committee, participation in the university library's CAS Online program, training engineering students participating in a reference desk peer program, and providing practicing engineers an opportunity to search through an Engineering Summer Conference. In addition, the process was explored beyond engineering through a semi-annual campuswide faculty workshop on bibliographic databases for the Center on Research, Teaching, and Learning. Each project contributed information that resulted in the modification of teaching techniques or dispelled assumptions. In view of the Engineering College goals described above, personal access to databases seemed a natural evolution in online systems. It provided an opportunity to integrate bibliographic databases into the college's educational process. Lack of funding through the university library system for end-user activity, however, has precluded expansion of some programs with the exception of the current CAS Online project for chemical engineering faculty. It is not the purpose of this presentation to review specific results from any one program. Instead the purpose is to indicate the issues that arose as the result of our experience, and how they may change the focus for end-user activity and training.

LENGTH AND EXTENT OF END-USER TRAINING

In general, online training for library staff has evolved into a complex procedure comprised of intensive workshops in basic skills or professional instruction by database vendors. This training is followed by in-house monitoring to reinforce the training and thus increase the skill level. Online practice and feedback from the supervisor has been considered important to monitor progress and increase technical proficiency. Experienced searchers also provide introductions to new bases and assist the novice in understanding the database architecture or philosophy. In-house training may be supplemented by semester-long, information and library studies courses. The goal for these programs is to produce searchers who can execute high quality online searches that meet the patron's needs.

The faculty/student end-user views the process as an adjunct to their information gathering activities and are usually not willing to allot large segments of time to refining their skills. Engineers are pragmatic researchers. The basis for their motivation is driven by a "need-to-know" and not on developing database expertise. Minimal

time is alloted by faculty to library staff for training, both for themselves and their students. One class hour is a very typical time limit. Often they may also expect more library instruction to be included in the lecture. Librarians willingly take advantage of any opportunity to teach information skills and will therefore compress a large quantity of information into the available time frame. This process limits the opportunities to build skills and to have someone monitor their progress. Difficulties arise in remembering protocol due to infrequent access of the systems after initial lectures. Even the well-motivated end-user with sophisticated searching skills will generally not have the need to search very often. And yet practice is necessary to maintain the skills.[1] Within these limited parameters, the practical goals might center on educating the library user in the availability of online resources and exposing them to the principles of the interactive process through "hands-on" experience.[2] If our experience in training professional searchers is valid, then quality searching demands indepth training in order to perform complex searches with optimal results. Training programs for end-users and the level of skill expected need to be in concert with well-defined goals. The level of expectation needs to be clearly expressed to the end-users in the program in order to avoid disillusionment with search results.

End-user searching is still in its infancy. It is still not clear why many patrons seem to discontinue searching once the initial enthusiasm has waned. Several government and industrial research libraries with financial resources, equipment, and administrative support have attempted end-user programs. In spite of the resources available to produce the programs, they are not experiencing heavy use of database systems even when they are hardwired or networked within laboratory areas.

Traditionally, reference librarianship has relied on the interview as the heart of the reference process in identifying the patron's real needs. The interrogation process involves illuminating, elaborating, questioning, and evaluating in managing the patron's problem and in determining its complexity. It is not appropriate to assume that the patron, whether student or faculty, is always certain of his or her information needs.

That analytical process has been adapted by the intermediary in determining the search strategy. Dolan and Kremin[3] define skills applicable to analyzing searches as a "cognitive style" in which concept analysis, flexibility of thinking, ability to think in synonyms, and anticipation of variant word forms and spellings are the keys to quality searching. In 1983, the University Library's Task Force on Online Evaluation drafted a Quality Assurance Program. It identified basic, desirable searcher skills or competencies: breaks down question into its components; separates essential concepts from extraneous information; recognizes discrete, overlapping, and unrelated concepts; constructs logical search formulations; formulates alternate strategies; translates user's terminology into preferred vocabulary of the database to be searched.

Problem analysis is a complex task that may be critical to the success of end-user searching. An online system will not solve broad, poorly defined problems. Students who participated in the semester-long class mentioned above have traditionally performed online searches after spending a significant portion of the term identifying a wide variety of research topics. In the course of the process, they redefined their original search problem. In a recent term, students could choose to conduct their search at a point earlier in the term. Those who chose to search earlier expressed less satisfaction with the online experience.

Patrons with good deductive reasoning and analytical skills can quickly apply them to abstract ideas. Those searchers who have demonstrated strong deductive traits seem to be attracted to searching online systems and are most often satisfied with the results. Defining the essential concepts is a confusing process for the average patron. Simple searches may lack essential elements. In addition, the skill should be expanded to the interactive process to include the ability to digest information while inputing new information.

"The searcher does need to be constantly reformulating the list of options and contingencies. The ability to do this quickly can make a difference not just in terms of efficiency of the search but in its effectiveness.[4] There is a critical need to teach effective methods of problem solving in order to assist the end-user in articulating and defining their search questions. The educator must develop a feedback mechanism so the process can be reinforced when new information needs arise.

DEVELOPING REALISTIC EXPECTATIONS FOR THE DATABASE SYSTEMS

Library literature is quick to promote the number of databases available to demonstrate the broad capacity of the systems. The latest statistics from Cuadra Associates indicates that there are now over two thousand databases available. In addition, libraries today can easily boast that they have access to several systems with hundreds of files.

Patrons need to be made aware of the vast and unusual resources available on these systems. However, a search specialist's knowledge of the actual capabilities of those information resources can differ vastly from the expectations of the patrons. Students today have high expectations of database systems. They assume that anything that is computerized will yield high-quality results. InfoTrac's laser disk system, which is accessed through microcomputers in the university's undergraduate library, seems indicative of that assumption. It is extremely popular with the students despite the fact that it is limited in its interactive techniques and lacks the power of Boolean logic.

We also need to dispel the assumption that library information is "better" when it is computerized. Patrons must be encouraged to seek assistance from professionals when the search is not successful, in order to avoid the assumption that information is not available, because they have not found it with their search strategy.[5] The degree of online searching experience appears to have an impact on the user's information-seeking behavior. End-users often have little awareness that they possess limited or unrefined searching abilities, and that they may not be optimizing the system's capabilities.

CONTINUING EDUCATION

The online professional has a responsibility to remain current in the field by reviewing changes in the system protocol and by exploring the capabilities of new bases or modifications in reloaded bases. Supplier or vendor database descriptions for new files often contain slightly exaggerated advertising claims; at other times there are significant omissions of capabilities that may be valuable for a particular patron.

Professionals also may explore databases for their interdisciplinary applications. Volumes of literature arrive almost daily in the form of newsletters, guidesheets, and advertisements, which require scanning to ferret out information relevant to a subject specialty. It presently seems unclear how end-users can be motivated to continually update their knowledge of new files or how willing they will be to modify their search techniques to take advantage of new software capability.

IMPLICATIONS AND APPLICATIONS OF END-USER SEARCHING

Our professional literature reflects the complexity of online databases and the concern for producing valid, meaningful results through indepth training of the online specialist. Notwithstanding that fact, however, we have felt the obligation through the reference process to educate patrons in new information resources. User education is designed to assist students and faculty in developing skills that will make them more independent in handling their information needs.

Personal access to online systems has been quickly accepted as another aspect of the educational process. Vendored user-friendly systems, such as BRS/After Dark and Knowledge Index, which are promoted directly to the end-user, have created additional pressures for librarians to be involved in end-user activities.

However, the experience we have gained in developing training programs for new professional searchers should provide some caveats and assist in the development of some well-defined goals in setting the direction for end-user training.

End-user searching will provide the opportunity for librarians to increase and strengthen their role as educators and as consultants in the information process. In some cases the program has served as a catalyst in allowing classroom time for library lectures where there had previously been resistance on the part of the faculty. Patrons know their research subject best and therefore may feel they would be happier with managing their own results. While we are looking at how we can train end-users, we should also be looking at how they currently access and handle information. Traditional card catalogs and standard indexes were designed with inflexible guidelines. Online systems are malleable with far greater access capability. We should not always try to change the patron's behavior as we have done in the past, but instead consider creative ways in which we can integrate these systems into their information gathering process.

An educational program should include more than search strategy and skills, but also should make patrons aware of the capabilities, the complexity of online systems, and their potential pitfalls. Once they have received a clear presentation of the fundamental issues they can then determine the extent to which they want to be involved in the process. Any end-user request for advice on search strategy or database selection provides the information specialist with additional educational opportunities for refining end-user skills.

Some patrons may choose to rely on an intermediary to perform more complex searches. User education, which provides experiences with the systems, should result in more clearly defined search requests. As search statements improve, search results are more likely to be within the realm of expectations.

A well-defined end-user program could lead to better understanding of the intermediary's role in complex searches and stimulate demand for advice from library staff with expertise. At the same time it could free the specialist from executing searches for simple information needs. Ultimately, it serves to strengthen our rapport with faculty and students in meeting their information needs.

NOTES

1.   D. Case, "End User Searching May Lead to Growth in Librarians," *Advanced Technology Libraries* 14 (9) (September 1985): 1,8.

2.   Sandra Ward and L.M. Osegueda, "Teaching University Student End-Users about Online Searching," *Science & Technology Librarian* 5 (Fall 1984): 17-31.

3.   Donn R. Dolan and Michael C. Kremin, "The Quality Control of Search Analysts," *Online* 3 (April 1979): 8-16.

4.   Randolph E. Hock, "Who Should Search?: The Attributes of a Good Searcher," In *Online Searching Techniques and Management* (Chicago: ALA, 1983).

5.   Janet L. Chapman, "A State Transition Analysis of Online Information-Seeking Behavior," *American Society for Information Science Journal* (September 1981): 325-333.

WHAT'S ON THE FISH?

Journal Article:

AN ACCESSION NUMBER: 23412. 8505.
PT PUBLICATION TYPE: Journal Article.
AU AUTHOR/S: Siegler-Ilene-C. George-Linda-K.
TI TITLE: Sex differences in coping and perceptions of l
SO SOURCE: Journal of Geriatric Psychiatry. 1983. Vol.
      p. 197-209. (13p.).
YR YEAR: 1983.
DE DESCRIPTORS: Attitudes. Males. Females. Sex-Dif
      Coping-Behavior. Emotions. Life-Cycle. Stress.
ID IDENTIFIERS: Locus of Control.
AB ABSTRACT: Sex differences in coping and perception
      explored during the fifth examination r   resp
      and 50 women) of the Duke Second
      interviews, men described the
      and as more acti

IMPLIED CONCEPT

Lowest Posted Concept

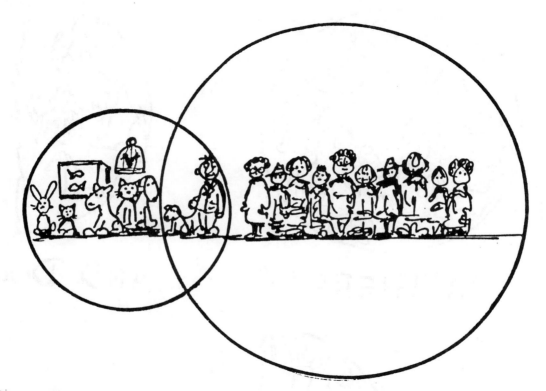

Pet Therapy   AGED

SUCCESSIVE FRACTIONS

PET THERAPY

AND DOGS

AND 1980-PRESENT

1/2/1
631072   85156072
Pet therapy evaluated. The Kingsmead cats.
Newberry SR
Geriatr Nur (London) (ENGLAND),Jan 1985,
 5 (1) p7-9,   ISSN 0262-5024
Tags: Animal; Human
Descriptors: *Aged--Psychology (PX);

 *Bonding, Human-Pet; *Cats; *Object

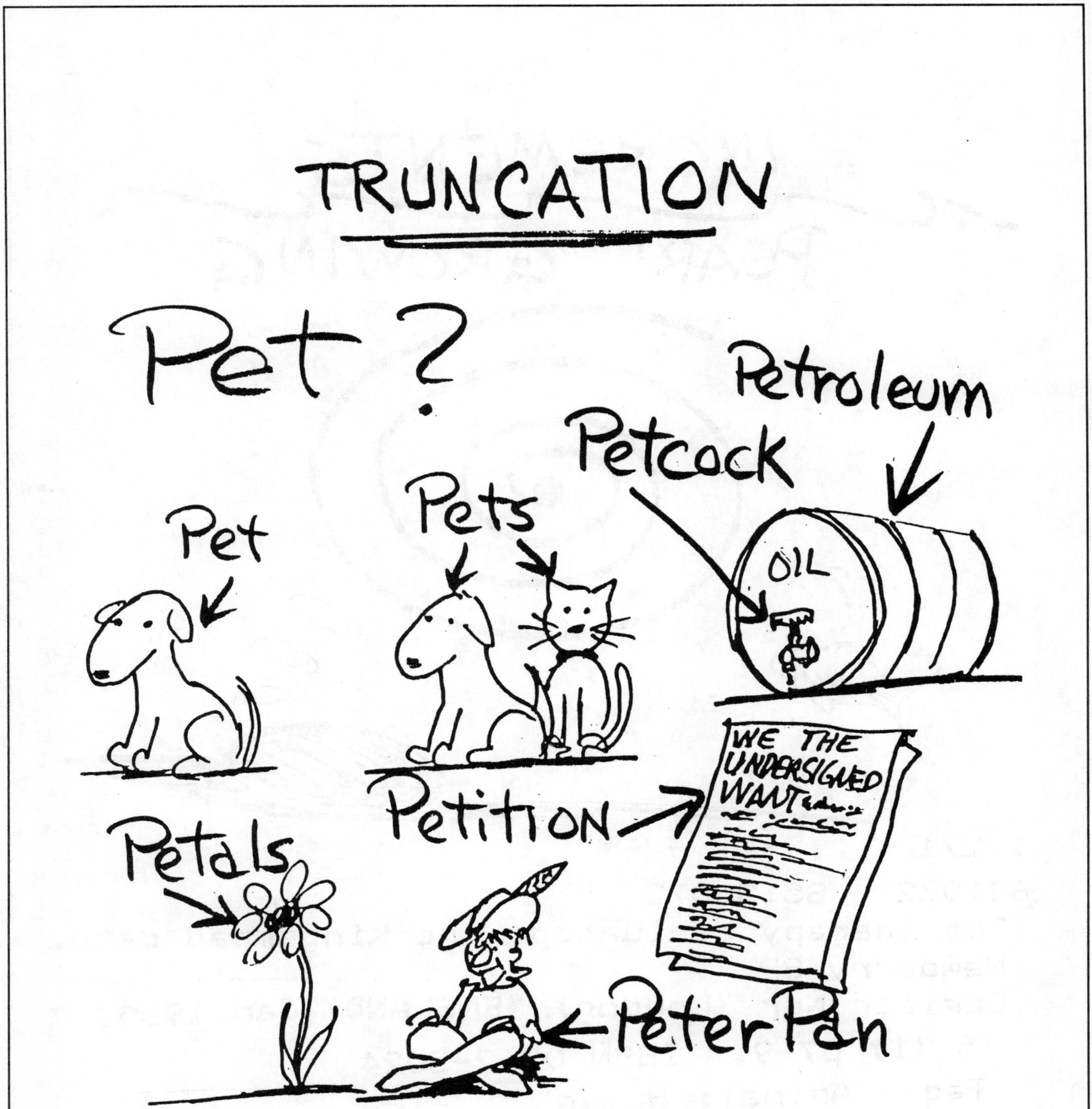
TRUNCATION
Pet ?
Petroleum
Petcock
Pets
Pet
OIL
WE THE UNDERSIGNED WANT
Petition
Petals
Peter Pan

NESTING

PETS AND (AGED OR ELDERLY)

? DOGS OR CATS
   3 DOCUMENTS

? DOGS AND CATS
   1 DOCUMENT

? DOGS NOT CATS
   1 DOCUMENT

ADJUSTING
RECALL AND PRECISION

RECALL -- Percentage of relevant items
retrieved by search

PRECISION-- Percentage of retrieved items
relevant to the search
topic

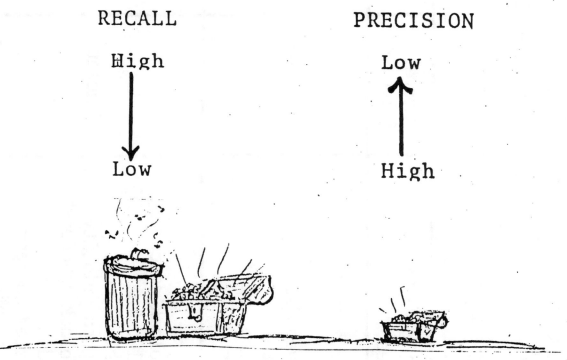

RECALL

High

Low

PRECISION

Low

High

High recall usually implies low precision

ADJUSTING RECALL AND PRECISION

	To increase recall		To increase precision
Database Selection	Search all possible databases		Search most appropriate database(s) Use DIALINDEX
Strategy	Broaden or extend a concept Use more general concepts Reduce number of concepts		Narrow a concept Use specific concepts or assign priorities Increase number of concepts
Concepts	Building block concepts of equal value Building block concepts of assigned priority Building block concepts modified Lowest posted concept Implied concepts Increments		Building block concepts of equal value Building block concepts of assigned priority Building block concepts modified Lowest-posted concept Successive fractions

```
PRESS      TO SELECT

   1   EasyNet-I   We pick the database
   2   EasyNet-II  You pick the database
   H   Help
Total charges thus far :      $0.00
-> 1
```

```
PRESS      TO SELECT

   1   Subject
   2   Person
   3   Place
   4   Organization
   H   Help
Total charges thus far :      $0.00
-> 1
```

```
PRESS      TO SELECT

   1   Current Events
   2   Business, Economics
   3   Sci/Tech, Computers, Medicine
   4   Law, Trademarks, Patents
   5   Social sciences, Education
   6   Art, Literature and Entertainment
   7   Religion, Philosophy
   H   Help
Total charges thus far :      $0.00
-> 3
```

```
PRESS      TO SELECT
```

```
    1   Agriculture
    2   Biology
    3   Chemistry
    4   Engineering, technology, computer
    5   Earth sciences, energy
    6   Mathematics, physics
    7   Medicine, allied health
    H   Help
Total charges thus far :     $0.00
-> 7
```

```
PRESS      TO SELECT
```

```
    1   Medicine
    2   Nursing and allied health
    3   Pharmacology
    H   Help
Total charges thus far :     $0.00
```

```
    -> 2
```

```
   PRESS      TO SELECT

    1   Professional journals
    2   Popular magazines
    3   Newsletters on allied health
    4   Books on nursing and allied health
    5   Encyclopedias
    6   List of related databases
    H   Help
 Total charges thus far :     $0.00
 -> 2
```

```
PRESS      TO SELECT

  1   Bibliography (references only)
  2   Full-text article
  H   Help
Total charges thus far :      $0.00
-> 1



Enter your specific topic.

(type H for important examples)
    or B to back up)

-> PET THERAPY AND NURSING HOMES

Is:
PET THERAPY AND NURSING HOMES
  Correct ? (Yes/No) -> Y
```

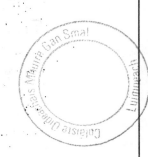

```
Occurrence   Search expression
----------   ------------------
       833   PET
      1511   THERAPY
         4   PET THERAPY
       580   NURSING
      4088   HOMES
       225   NURSING HOMES
```

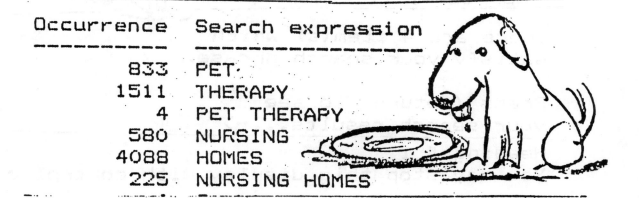

```
   Nothing was retrieved.   No charge.
   Press (return) to continue...->
```

```
If you wish, you may type
SOS for online human assistance
with your search.
Press (return) to continue...->


PRESS    TO SELECT

  1   Bibliography (references only)
  2   Full-text article
  H   Help
Total charges thus far :    $0.00
-> 1
```

```
Enter your specific topic.

 (type H for important examples)
    or B to back up)

-> PET THERAPY

 Is:
PET THERAPY
 Correct ? (Yes/No) -> Y
```

```
There are 4 item(s) which
satisfy your search phrase.


Press (return) to see
your search results...->
```

```
Heading # 1
You may stop this display with control c

1967866    DATABASE: MI File 47
   Pet therapy for heart and soul.
   Pechter, Kerry
   Prevention   v37  p80(7)  Aug  1985
   CODEN: PRNEA
Press (return) to continue...->
```

Indexing Listing for: AGELINE — DESCRIPTORS

No.	Field	Term
17	DE	PETS
67	DE	PHARMACEUTICAL ... IC...
17	DE	PHARMACISTS
4	DE	PHILIPPINES
1	DE	PHOTOGRAPHS
73	DE	PHYSICAL ACTIVITY
24	DE	PHYSICAL CHARACTERISTICS
341	DE	PHYSICAL CONDITION
69	DE	PHYSICAL MOBILITY
30	DE	PHYSICAL PERFORMANCE
51	DE	PHYSICAL THERAPY
91	DE	PHYSICALLY HANDICAPPED
52	DE	PHYSICIAN EDUCATION
12	DE	PHYSICIAN FEES
99	DE	PHYSICIAN PATIENT RELATIONS
134	DE	PHYSICIAN SERVICES
39	DE	PHYSICIAN VISITS
299	DE	PHYSICIANS
3	DE	PHYSICIANS ASSISTANTS
1	DE	PITUITARY GLAND
3	DE	PLACEBOS
34	DE	PLANNING AND SERVICE AREAS
1	DE	PLUMBING

ENTER DATABASE NAME_: AARP

* COPYRIGHT 1985 AMERICAN ASSOCIATION

OF RETIRED PERSONS

BRS SEARCH MODE - ENTER QUERY
     1_: | PET ADJ THERAPY

     RESULT   8 DOCUMENTS
     2_: | ..PRINT 2 BIBL/DOC =1-8

          1

AN ACCESSION NUMBER: 23450. 8509.
PT PUBLICATION TYPE: Monograph.
AU AUTHOR/S: McLeod-Cappy.
TI TITLE: Animals in the nursing home:
SO SOURCE: Cappy McLeod, Colorado Springs
          2   1981.   (

```
File 411:DIALINDEX(tm)
(Copr. DIALOG Inf.Ser.Inc.)
?SF 1, 218,154,47,111,37


File    1: ERIC - 66-86/JAN
File 218: Nursing & Allied Health (CINAHL)
File 154: MEDLINE - 80-86/FEB
File  47: MAGAZINE INDEX - 1959-MAR 1970,
File 111: NATIONAL NEWSPAPER INDEX - 79-86
File  37: SOCIOLOGICAL ABSTRACTS - 63-85/1
File           Items   Description
-----          -----   -----------

?S PET(W)THERAPY AND NURSING(W)HOME?

    1: ERIC - 66-86/JAN
             192   PET
            6425   THERAPY
               3   PET(W)THERAPY
            3202   NURSING
           18778   HOME?
             478   NURSING(W)HOME?
               2   PET(W)THERAPY
                   AND NURSING(W)HOME?
  218: Nursing & Allied Health (CINAHL)-83-8
              11   PET
            4617   THERAPY
               3   PET(W)THERAPY
           11176   NURSING
             125   HOME?
             275   NURSING(W)HOME?
               0   PET(W)THERAPY
                   AND NURSING(W)HOME?
```

WHERE AM I?

```
File 218:Nursing & Allied Health
(c. CINAHL Corp. 1985)(CINAHL)-83-85/Oct

          Set    Items   Description
          ---    -----   -----------
?S PET(W)THERAPY

                  11     PET
                4617     THERAPY
          S1       3     PET(W)THERAPY
?TYPE S1/7/1


  1/7/1
0041424
    Pet therapy with terminal cancer patient
    Muschel IJ
    SOC CASEWORK, 1984 Oct; 65(8): 451-8
    Doc Type: research          (15 ref)
?TYPE S1/5/2
```

```
File 154:MEDLINE - 80-86/FEB

        Set    Items    Description
        ---    -----    -----------
?S PET(W)THERAPY


            506    PET
         271194    THERAPY
        S1       3    PET(W)THERAPY
?TYPE S1/2/1-3


 1/2/1
1631072    85156072
  Pet therapy evaluated. The Kingsmead cats
  Newberry SR
  Geriatr Nur (London) (ENGLAND)    ,Jan 198
    5 (1) p7-9,    ISSN 0262-5024
    Journal Code: GES
  Languages: ENGLISH
  Journal Announcement: 8507
  Subfile: Nursing
  Tags: Animal; Human
  Descriptors:  *Aged--Psychology (PX);

   *Bonding, Human-Pet; *Cats; *Object
```

Online Bibliographic Instruction
for Business Classes

Ronald P. Colman

The purpose was to inform both under-graduate and graduate students in the College of Business about online database searching. One of the required classes for all business students is Business Information Systems offered by the Department of Operations Research and Information Systems. Personal contact was made with the instructor in each class section to schedule a one-hour BI search demonstration.

Handouts and overheads were used in each class to illustrate how a database is selected and a search is prepared using thesauri and Boolean logic. Each class was then asked to suggest a topic, and a brief online search was done. Twenty-five-inch monitors were connected to our micro-computer enabling the entire class to observe the step-by-step search procedure, which included downloading as well as printing the results.

There was a noticeable increase in enthusiasm by teaching faculty and students for the "live" search demonstrations over the previous exclusive use of transparencies to illustrate sample searches. Many students come back later to have their own searches done. There has been a significant increase in the total number of searches done, especially for students. Another result is the increased use of interlibrary loan. A less tangible result is increased respect for the library faculty by teaching faculty and students.

Teaching End-User Searching
to Health Professionals

Alice C. Wygant

The "Basics of Searching MEDLINE" is a
seven-hour course designed by the National Library
of Medicine (NLM) for end-users. NLM trains the
instructors and publishes the text, *The Basics of
Searching MEDLINE: A Guide for the Health Professional*.   The Moody Medical Library began
teaching this class in May 1985.   Classes have
been held monthly since that time.   This session
deals with the mechanics of setting up the class
and with the materials and teaching methods used
in the class. It will also cover some of the special
problems and benefits of developing an end-user
searching program in a large, academic medical
center.

Interdisciplinary Bibliographic
Instruction in Linguistics:
Reinforcement through Online
Searching and Parallel Logic

Edmund F. SantaVicca

The purpose of the project was two-fold: 1) to deliver bibliographic instruction (BI) to students and faculty whose information needs cut across academic disciplines; 2) to expand the market for BI and online searching in the humanities. The target audience was comprised of students and faculty from the Departments of English, Modern Languages, Communications, Psychology, Philosophy, and Education. Announcement was made through flyers, memoranda, and personal contact.

Online searching in linguistics was explained and demonstrated, with a focus on strategies of parallel logic, for example, organization of the discipline/organization of printed reference information systems/user definition of information needs/access classification systems and subject headings/Boolean and other manipulations of online systems (using DIALOG cluster of bases in the humanities).

Free online searches of ERIC and MLA Bibliography were provided for instruction-related topics. Evaluations registered enthusiasm of participants. Immediate follow-up searches were requested, as well as a request to add an additional class section for BI. Plans call for repetition of this advanced session each academic term.

INTERDISCIPLINARY BIBLIOGRAPHIC INSTRUCTION IN LINGUISTICS:
REINFORCEMENT THROUGH ON-LINE SEARCHING AND PARALLEL LOGIC

Edmund F. SantaVicca, Humanities Reference Bibliographer

Cleveland State University Libraries
1860 East 22nd St., Cleveland, OH 44114

The purpose of the project was two-fold: 1) to deliver
BI to students and faculty whose information needs cut
across academic disciplines; 2) to expand the market for
BI and on-line searching in the Humanities. The target
audience was comprised of students and faculty of Departments of English, Modern Languages, Communications,
Psychology, Philosophy and Education. Announcement was
made through flyers, memoranda and personal contact.

On-line searching in linguistics was explained and demonstrated, with a focus on strategies of parallel logic,
i.e., organization of the discipline/organization of
printed reference information systems/user definition of
information needs/access classification systems and subject headings/Boolean and other manipulations of on-line
systems (using DIALOG cluster of bases in the Humanities).

Free on-line searches of ERIC and MLA Bibliography
were provided, for instruction-related topics. Evaluations
registered enthusiasm of participants. Immediate follow-up
searches were requested, as well as a request to add an
additional class section for BI. Plans call for repetition
of this advanced session each academic term.

Online Searching Guides:

Discussion Group Handouts
and Sample Materials
from the LOEX
Clearinghouse Collection

BARUCH COLLEGE

EXERCISES IN ONLINE BIBLIOGRAPHIC SEARCHING - COLLEGE FRESHMEN

Topics for students:

   1. Locate linguistics articles on Black English dialects.

   2. Claims of Argentina and Great Britain on the Falklands (or Malvinas)

   3. Compare population trends in Asia and Africa.

   4. Historical studies of women's participation in revolutions.

Tools:

   Catalog of data bases with broad subject access and descriptions

   Several thesaurus sets

   Venn diagrams are used to test logic

Students to work in small groups to prepare an online search request

Their work is reviewed by college librarians/search specialists.

Well-planned searches are run as demonstrations. Some generate off line printouts.

ARGENTINA'S and GREAT BRITAIN'S CLAIMS ON THE FALKLAND ISLANDS (OR MALVINAS)

Databases:

1. File #111   National Newspaper Index (I.A.C.)
2. File #211   Newsearch I.A.C.)
3. File # 49   PAIS International
4. File # 39   Historical Abstracts
5. File # 37   Sociological Abstracts
6. File # 90   Economics Abstracts International
7. File # 84   PTS International Times Series
8. File # 83   PAT International Forecasts

Terms: Argentina, Great Britian, Falkland Islands

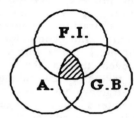   Falkland Islands and Argentina, and

Falkland Islands and Great Britain

Falkland Islands or Malvinas

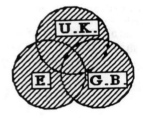

England or Great Britain or United Kingdom

   Falkland Islands not United States involvement:

Do not use- student already has 3 terms
Eliminating the U.S. would cost alot of time and money

Baruch College

DATABASE CONNECTIONS

PREPARING YOUR SEARCH STRATEGY

ABOUT YOUR SEARCH STRATEGY

If you plan to research your topic using databases available through the **Database Connection**, you will need to prepare a search strategy. There are four basic steps:

1. Describe your research topic.
2. Decide which database you are going to search.
3. Decide which keywords and subject headings best describe your topic.
4. Be prepared to modify your strategy. This may mean re-examing your topic, using a different database, or changing the keywords and subject headings you use.

These are the same steps you follow when you use print sources such as the card catalog or an index.

WHY BOTHER

Your search strategy:

o Helps you anticipate what terms are best used to describe the different aspects that make up your research topic

o Ensures that you are using the right database to find the information you need

o Ensures that you locate exactly the information you need, not a lot of extraneous information that you will have to sift through and discard

o Ensures that you can make the best use of your time on the computer

AVOID THE DISADVANTAGES

Computers have many powerful options, but they can produce very poor results. For example, if you asked to see bibliographic citations containing the word "pigment," the computer will not give you citations containing the words "pigments," even though the articles were related. By taking a few minutes to plan your search strategy, you will avoid many of the computer's disadvantages and be able to use its many advantages.

TIME IS NOT ON YOUR SIDE

When you use print sources, you are free to use them for as long as you need in order to identify the information you need. The only limitation is your paper's due date. When you use the **Database Connection**, you have one half-hour to complete and print your search results. Therefore, you will need to make decisions quickly about which terms you want to use and in what combinations. You will be prepared to do this, if you have planned your search strategy.

USE THE WORKSHEET

The back of this handout describes the steps for preparing your search strategy. You will also need the Database Connection handouts Worksheet for the Database Connection and Databases Available on BRS/After Dark. These, and other helpful Database Connection handouts, can be found in the stand near the elevator on Main Level. If you need help with your search strategy, please ASK at the Reference Desk (Main Level).

STEP 1: Describe your research topic. Write a sentence or question that describes your research topic. Be sure that your sentence or question includes all the important aspects (or concepts) of your topic. For example, the research topic "the role of the Catholic Church in Brazillian politics" has 3 different concepts; Catholic Church, Brazil, and politics.

Search Hint: Print indexes are an important source to help you refine your search strategy. They will provide additional terms and phrases you may not have thought of, and they will also give you a sense of how much is being published on your research topic.

STEP 2: Decide which database you are going to search. Be prepared to enter this information into the computer at the beginning of your search. To do this, study the Database Connections handout <u>Databases Available on BRS/After Dark</u> and select the two most appropriate databases (one is reserved as a backup) for your research topic . **You will need both the subject category and the four-letter database label** for each database. For example, the above topic could be searched in **PAIS** and **RELI**; both databases are in the **Social Sciences** subject category.

STEP 3a: Decide which keywords and subject headings best describe your topic. Begin by transferring the different concepts that make up your research topic to the concept grid (one concept per box). Keep your search simple; limit yourself to no more than 2-3 concepts. Make sure that each concept is a different aspect of your topic.

Under each concept add any subject headings (use the database thesaurus to identify these), keywords, jargon words, examples of , or phrases that may be used to describe that concept.

Search Hint: Phrases such as "the effects of" and the "unique aspects of" <u>cannot</u> be seached with a computer. However, specific effect (for example, increased aggression) <u>can</u> be searched.

STEP 3b: Select the most important terms under each concept. You will begin your search by using the most important words under each concept. The other words should be used to modify your search, if the original search strategy does not produce the results you expected.

STEP 3c: Decide which words need to be truncated so that you will retrieve different forms of the same word.

Search Hint: You will enter terms into the computer concept box-by-concept box. The connector OR is used between the words **within** a concept box. The connector AND is used **between** different concept boxes.

STEP 4: Be prepared to modify your strategy. Most searches produce unexpected results: too many citations, too few citations, zero citations, or citations that are not about your topic even though all the words you requested are present. Because you only have one half-hour to complete your search, plan how you will modify your search strategy. You may want to consult the Database Connections handout. <u>Analyzing and Modifying Your Search Results.</u>

Bucknell University

WORKSHEET
FOR THE DATABASE CONNECTION   Bucknell University

(To be used with the <u>Database Connection Workbook</u> or the Database Connections handout: <u>Preparing Your Search Strategy</u>)

Step 1-- Describe your search topic:

_____

_____

_____

_____

Step 2--Select an appropriate database:

   Subject category: _____

      Database label: _____

   Subject category: _____

      Database label: _____

Step 3--Develop your search strategy:

CONCEPT 1	CONCEPT 2	CONCEPT 3
OR	OR	OR
OR	OR	OR
OR	OR	OR
OR	OR	OR
(AND)	(AND)	

Step 4--Plan possible modifications to your search strategy:

Frequently your original search strategy will not produce the results you expect. Be prepared to modify your search strategy using the ideas below. If your original search strategy produces:

   few citations use:
      -additional synonyms under each concept; broader terms for
         concepts; truncate more terms.

   many citations use:
      -fewer synonyms under each concept; narrower terms for concepts;
         truncate fewer terms.

   zero citations:
      -check for spelling errors; check that you have used connectors
         (AND, OR) correctly; use suggestions for "few citations" above.

   For more help, see the Database Connections handout: <u>Analyzing and
      Modifying Your Search Results</u>.

Bucknell University

QUICK REFERENCE GUIDE

To Combine Concepts:
   OR

                          Use to **Broaden** your search strategy. i.e., each document must contain **at least one** of the terms you have listed.

   AND

                          Use to **Narrow** your search strategy. i.e., each document must contain **all** of the terms you have listed.

To Search a Word Stem:
  Truncation:

     educate$**   Add the truncation symbol ($) to the stem word (for example, **educat) to retrieve more than one form of a word when they are used interchangeably. e.g., educat**e**, educat**es**, educat**ion**, etc.

SEARCH COMMANDS

                                                      ENTER:

To **Change** database   **C**
    Use this command when you want to change databases

To return to the **Main Menu**   **M**
    Use this command when you want to change subject areas

To return to the **Search** mode   **S**
    Use this command to return to the search mode after you have been in display mode

To **Display** documents   **D**
    Documents may be displayed in five different formats
        ti-- title field only
        s(hort)--author, title, date, volume/issue, page
          number fields
        L(ong)--all fields
        td--tailored display-you specify which fields

To **Review** the search questions and answers you have   **R**
      already entered

To log **OFF** BRS/After Dark (exit)   **O**

For more help, see the Database Connections handout: <u>Advanced Searching Techniques</u> (available at the Reference Desk).

Bucknell University

CALIFORNIA POLYTECHNIC STATE UNIVERSITY LIBRARY
San Luis Obispo

Library 301   Spring 1985
                          COURSE OUTLINE
                  Computerized Literature Searching

Instructors: Ilene Rockman (Coordinator), Eileen Pritchard, Jay Waddell,
                Wayne Montgomery, Sharon Fujitani, Lane Page

Audience: Juniors, seniors, and graduate students interested in enhancing
                their knowledge of library research skills.

Objectives: 1. To provide students with background information concerning
                    how information is organized and retrieved.

                2. To acquaint students with the principles of effective manual
                    search techniques using indexes and abstracts.

                3. To provide instruction in the use of computerized biblio-
                    graphic databases.

                4. To enable students to perform their own research strategy
                    using computerized bibliographic databases.

Class Schedule:

April 4   Introduction to the class, course requirements,   Ms. Rockman
                definitions of terms

April 11   Principles of manual searching in indexes and   Mr. Waddell
                abstracts,thesaurii, proper citation practices,
                explanation of manual search assignment

April 18   Function and use of thesaurii, indexing principles Mr. Montgomery
                applied to online searching, comparison of printed
                sources to online files, advantages and disadvan-
                tages of online searching. Week 2 homework due.

April 25   No class - Poly Royal

May 2   Instruction in terminal usage, basic commands   Ms. Fujitani
                and search strategies, assignment to subject
                specialist librarians. Distribution of take-
                home midterm. Week 3 homework is due.

May 9   Home searching with microcomputers. Distribution Ms. Rockman
                of online search forms and guidelines for final
                project. Take-home midterm is due.

California Polytechnic State University Library

May 16-30   Appointments with subject specialist librarians
             to formulate search strategies. Hands-on experiences
             with terminals to execute computer searches. It is
             your responsibility to make contact with a librarian
             once a week during this time. By May 30 you will
             receive a course evaluation form and questionnaire
             which are due on June 6.

June 6   Final project due. Subject-oriented discussion
             groups to exchange information and draw conclusions
             about search results.

Requirements

1. There is no required textbook for this course. Instead, students will be
    provided with handouts which will reinforce the material covered in lecture,
    and assist in preparing for the midterm, completing the written assignments,
    and compiling the final project.

2. A one-credit course has a limited number of class sessions, and each
    meeting is important; each involves the presentation of new information,
    and often, a new assignment. Therefore, you will be required to attend
    each class session.

3. On May 2, a take-home midterm will be distributed. Responses are to be
    typewritten, and are due the following week, May 9. You will not be
    permitted to operate the terminal and advance in the class unless you
    pass the midterm at the 70% mark.

4. At the end of the quarter, a final project is to be submitted on June 6.

Evaluation

Your total grade will be determined according to the following factors:

1. 20% will be based upon three citations and one annotation from the manual
    search exercises. These will be due on April 18 and May 2.

2. 25% will be based upon the take-home midterm due on May 9.

3. 55% will be based upon the final project due on June 6. This project should
    include an introductory statement, and 20 citations written in a consistent
    bibliographic format (1 of which is annotated) based upon both the manual
    and online searches. Your project should also include the complete online
    printout, search strategy log for manual searching, search strategy log
    for online searching, questionnaire, and evaluation form.

California Polytechnic State University Library

A BRIEF GUIDE TO DATABASE SEARCHING

WHEN SHOULD A DATABASE SEARCH BE DONE?

A database search is appropriate when the search is a well defined, narrow topic (usually when 50 to 100 or fewer citations will cover the topic) and involves two or more terms or sub-parts which can be matched on the computer, but not easily done in a manual search. A database search is especially appropriate for a research paper, senior project, or thesis requiring a thorough review of the literature.

A database search is not recommended when only a few sources are needed (not an extensive coverage of the literature) and when the sources are quickly and easily found in a printed index. A database search is not usually recommended when the sources are scattered among many printed indexes and disciplines, due to the expense of searching each database. Also in searching many disciplines, one must establish the vocabulary of each discipline before searching their databases.

WHAT DOES A DATABASE SEARCH DO?

A database search enables the requestor to get bibliographic citations that list journals with articles about his or her subject.

WHAT ARE THE RESULTS OF A DATABASE SEARCH?

A database search gives a printout of citations on the topic searched.

WHAT IS THE COST OF A DATABASE SEARCH?

The cost of a database search ranges from approximately five dollars to twenth-five dollars or more.

HOW LONG DOES A DATABASE SEARCH TAKE?

The time the requestor spends initiating the search is a few minutes. Observing the search (if the librarian requests an appointment) requires 20 to 60 minutes. Waiting for the search to be done and the prints to arrive at Interlibrary Loan takes about a week.

Note: The requestor should allow time to retrieve articles that are not in the Kennedy Library. The requestor may ask to get articles through Interlibrary Loan which arrive in about two weeks.

WHO TO SEE TO GET A SEARCH DONE

Go to the Reference Department and tell the librarian at the reference desk the subject you wish to search by computer. The person on duty will tell you the name of the librarian who will do the search and where to find that person. Before seeing the search librarian, fill out the blue Computer-Based Search Request Form which is available at the reference desk or in Interlibrary Loan. Read the reverse of this guide for recommendations for filling out the blue request form. If you have questions about what to say on the blue form, discuss them with your search librarian.

California Polytechnic State University Library

RECOMMENDATIONS FOR FILLING OUT THE BLUE
REQUEST FORM FOR A COMPUTER ASSISTED SEARCH:

_____ Before doing a computer assisted search, it is often useful to look for article citations on your subject in a printed index or abstracting service. (See the green list at the Reference Desk entitled <u>Abstracts and Indexes by Subject</u>. The abstracts and indexes which are both in printed form as well as searchable on computer are indicated with an asterisk in this list.) <u>A look at the printed indexes and abstracts can help you select the best files to search on computer. Also, it helps you identify the best search terms, and to narrow the focus of your topic, if appropriate.</u>

_____ On the blue form give a clear, accurate description of the topic <u>in sentence form</u> so the librarian can combine the terms logically. The sentence is essential.

In addition,

_____ a. Narrow the search. Avoid being too general.

_____ b. List all the key terms, synonyms, and variant spellings.

_____ c. Find additional terms in a dictionary or thesaurus.

Agriculture: A source that will list the scientific name if a plant or animal name is used. Common names should also be listed.

Biology: A source that will list the scientific name if a plant or animal name is used.

Chemistry: <u>Chemical Abstracts Index Guide</u> (behind the reference desk) to find the proper terms used in the database and the registry numbers for chemicals.

Education: <u>Thesaurus of ERIC Descriptors</u> (on the ERIC table in the Reference Department or on the Index Table in the Learning Resources and Curriculum Department)

Psychology: <u>Thesaurus of Psychological Index Terms</u>

WHERE TO PICK UP AND PAY FOR THE RESULTS OF THE SEARCH

The search results may be paid for in cash or with a check payable to "Cal Poly" at the time the search results are picked up at the Interlibrary Loan office, Library 112. <u>Once the search is completed, the requestor is obligated to pay for the search.</u>

POLICY STATEMENT: The Reference Department does online searching as time allows, at no cost, for the following purposes: 1. To verify a citation when part of the citation is known. 2. To find brief information or citations too current to be in reference books or indexes. 3. To find brief information available online, after not finding it in available reference sources.

California Polytechnic State University Library

ALBERT R. MANN LIBRARY
Cornell Univerity

Instruction in Online Searching of Bibliographic Databases

The Albert R. Mann Library, Cornell University, provides an instructional program consisting of several components within its Public Services Division. In addition to teaching methods of retrieving information manually from printed sources, a new component has been developed which instructs students in online searching of bibliographic databases. The instructional program aims to develop an understanding of concepts and problems in the organization and retrieval of information, and to teach specific skills in the utilization of both print and online information resources.

Librarians at Mann Library have been teaching students and faculty to perform their own computer searches on user-friendly systems since Summer, 1983. At first, classes were course-related and covered topics in nutrition, human services, agriculture and life sciences. These classes are now supplemented by open workshops in searching offered to the entire Cornell community. During a class session, participants learn how to construct a search strategy for their topic and how to execute a search on the BRS After Dark system. Subsequently, participants make an appointment to run their own searches on a library microcomputer with the guidance of a trained "coach." Practice searches for students in course-related classes are usually funded by college or department. Participants in open workshops pay for their own searching.

GOALS: To teach students skills and concepts necessary for searching bibliographic databases and ones which they can transfer to other online bibliographic databases; to motivate students to use online systems and approach them with confidence; to evaluate the effectiveness of the program in achieving its objectives.

OBJECTIVES: The following are objectives for students who have attended an instructional session on searching BRS After Dark and have performed a search with coaching.

I. Students can define a bibliographic database, can give an example of a database, and can describe the content of what is being searched on the BRS After Dark system.

II. Given a list and a brief description of available databases, students can choose one to three databases appropriate to their topic.

III. Given an appropriate thesaurus, students can choose relevant terms for their topic and can add free text words as needed.

IV. Students can contruct a logical search strategy for their topic by identifying subject concepts and using Boolean operators to link terms and manipulate sets.

V. Students can use an online menu to independently input their search strategy on a terminal or microcomputer and execute the steps needed to print out citations.

VI. Students can list advantages and disadvantages of computer searching as compared to a manual search and recognize conditions when a computer search is likely to be more effective than a manual search.

VII. Students can recognize situations in which their search performed on BRS After Dark needs to be supplemented by further computer searching and or expertise.

mac/jl/3/4/88

Cornell University, Albert R. Mann Library

SEARCHING COMPUTERIZED BIBLIOGRAPHIC DATABASES

I. **Explanation of database searching**

   A. *Types of databases*
      1. Bibliographic
      2. Non-bibliographic (directory, full-text, numeric)

   B. *Database formats*
      1. Compact disk (Agricola, ERIC or DISCLOSURE)
      2. Mainframe (local or remote)
      3. Access to databases (Mann search services and other options)
      4. Print equivalents
      5. Advantages and disadvantages of electronic information retrieval
         + Combines concepts, speed, access points, customized output, updates
         - Timeframe, cost, "finesse" needed, coverage

   C. *Database content*
      1. Records
      2. Fields (access points)

   D. *Interpreting output and locating materials*

II. **Search Procedure**

   A. *Articulate and identify the topic*

   B. *Choose a database*

   C. *Separate the search topic into discrete concepts*

   D. *Think of other words for the concepts and list them*
      1. Consult controlled vocabulary/thesauri
      2. Identify free-text key words
      3. Consider variations in word endings
         truncation (*, $, ?, #)
      4. Use special features such as qualification (e.g., trees.ti. or trees in ti)

   E. *Connect the concepts* (use logical operators AND, OR, NOT to relate terms/sets)

   F. *Enter search statements*
      (how to begin and end a search, correct typographic errors,
      move around in the file with function keys, page up/down, etc.)

   G. *Perform, evaluate and modify the search*
      Search systems will be demonstrated; hands-on practice occurs outside of class

   H. *Record the search results* (recalling, printing, downloading)

III. **Requirements for searching and procedures for appointments** (yellow sheet)
      Sign up for a search time at the Second Floor Reference Desk. A librarian will help you
      structure your first search.

Albert R. Mann Library, Cornell University, Ithaca, NY 14853-4301

Cornell University, Albert R. Mann Library

EASTERN MICHIGAN UNIVERSITY
UNIVERSITY LIBRARY

Searching Computer Databases: Advantages and Limitations

ADVANTAGES

(1)   **Computer database searches provide more ways to find relevant information than do searches of print information sources.**

In print sources, you are lead to information by a relatively small number of access points -- author names in an author index and perhaps 1 to 10 subject headings per item in a subject index. In computer databases, you can search not only these access points but also every other word or phrase in a data record as well, including, for example, every word in a title, abstract (if available), or author's address (if available).

(2)   **Computer database searches provide more search flexibility than do searches of print information sources.**

If the topic under investigation involves the relationship between two or more concepts or variables, for example, "How are microcomputers being used to improve the reading comprehension of elementary school students?", a computer can easily link these concepts and display only those records where they all appear together.

(3)   **Computer database searches provide results faster that do searches of print information sources.**

A computer search can uncover relevant information much more quickly than can a manual search of print sources.

(4)   **Computer database searches often provide more current information than do searches of print information sources.**

It is frequently the case that when both print and computer versions of an information source exist, the computer version will be available for searching before the print version is received.

(5)   **Computer database searches make information available which is not found in print sources.**

Some information sources are available only in computer-readable form and have no print equivalents. Other information sources are available in both print and computer-readable forms, but the computer version is enhanced and contains more information than the print version.

(6)   **Computer database searches make information sources available which are not physically located in a particular place.**

Eastern Michigan University

A computer search can bring to any location, for example, a home or office as well as a library, information sources that are not physically owned.

(7)   Computer database searches provide printed results.

The results of a computer search can be printed out on paper (or, if performed with a microcomputer, can be stored in computer-readable form for later manipulation), while the results of a manual search of print sources must be copied by hand and/or duplicating machine.

LIMITATIONS

(1)   Retrospective searching is limited with computer database searches compared to searches of print information sources.

Most computer databases do not cover materials farther back than about 1970. To gather information before this period, print sources often must be consulted.

(2)   Some topics cannot be searched effectively using a computer database.

A search on a broad topic such as "microcomputers in education" would reveal so much material that it would not often be effective to do it.

(3)   If a computer search is performed for you by another individual, for example, a librarian, your work schedule often has to be modified to accommodate that of the searcher.

Database searching in libraries is usually a service that is offered by appointment only. While you can walk into a library at 6:00 p.m. on a Friday night and search a print information source, such convenience is not typically available for searching computer databases (unless you subscribe to the search service and do the search yourself).

(4)   Browsing through information "not related" to a topic (and unexpectedly discovering useful material) is discouraged during computer database searches because of the monetary cost.

When searching print sources, excellent material is often discovered when skimming and browsing through information that is found on the way to or adjacent to the information you are seeking.

(5)   Computer database searches cost money.

However, the advantages of computer searching (for example, speed, flexibility, currency, etc.) often make the monetary expenditure cost effective.

KJS 7/87

Eastern Michigan University

A HELPING HAND

ONLINE SEARCHES
Pros and Cons
joy/8-85

PROS

The computer quickly and efficiently cross-references multiple terms.

The computer can search authors, titles, subjects, sources, dates as well as abstracts and <u>texts</u> of material in a single operation.

Online searching can save hours of time.

Online searching offers greater flexibility in some instances, particularly when a search involves new concepts and jargon.

Printout of material located by the computer is portable, neat, and fairly easy to use.

Online searching may sometimes provide more recent information than can be found in printed indexes and abstracts.

Database suppliers are constantly increasing search capabilities.

CONS

It is almost impossible to manually cross-reference multiple terms efficiently and involves hundreds of man hours.

Printed versions of databases do not offer text searching. <u>Some</u> have abstracts but searching them involves extra steps in the search process and actual reading of the abstracts.

Computer searching may be expensive. Manual searching of printed indexes costs <u>only</u> time.

The computer cannot think. It is programmed to search words and subjects in only a fairly limited number of combinations.
1. Be aware that while the topic being searched may be "White socialworkers' stereotyped concepts of black clients," the computer is just as likely to pull articles on "Black clients stereotyped concepts of white socialworkers."

2. The computer searches abstract concepts such as "relationship to" or "effect of" with difficulty.

IF IN DOUBT ABOUT HAVING A COMPUTER SEARCH ON A TOPIC,

ASK A LIBRARIAN!

Gardner Webb College

DATABASE SEARCHING AT FENWICK LIBRARY

Fenwick Library offers access to a variety of computer databases which contain bibliographic citations for books, journal articles and other information sources. In most cases the information in the database corresponds to a printed index or catalog in the library. In an online search you search the database interactively and produce a list of information sources.

Searching a database in general enables you to:

1. cut through large amounts of information quickly
2. find materials that cover two or more topics
3. find words that are not used as subject headings in indexes.

Be aware that an online database search is <u>not</u> usually the best first step in research. A good online search requires that you prepare by:

1. doing some general reading on your topic to identify important concepts, terms, names, and dates.
2. looking at the subject headings in the printed version of the index or a thesaurus to the index to find out what terms are used in the database to describe your topic.

<u>DATABASE SERVICES FOR INFORMATION ABOUT BOOKS</u>:

<u>ALIS</u>:

What	- Fenwick Library's online catalog contains information about books, audiovisual materials, and microforms at Fenwick.
How	- Self-instructional database. It's free. Terminals are located in the reference area. - Use the <u>Library of Congress Subject Headings</u> books to determine which subject words are used.
Advantage	- Tells you whether an item is checked out or on reserve. - Finds books by author or title quickly.
Disadvantage	- Subject searching is sometimes cumbersome; ask at the reference desk for assistance. - Does not include journal articles.
Subjects best served	- The subjects taught at GMU.

George Mason University

OCLC:

What   – A union catalog of over 3,000 libraries in the U.S.

How   – It's free. Located near the reference desk. Bring the author or
                  title and ask a reference librarian to show you how to use it.

Advantage   – Tells which library owns a book, journal, score, etc.

Disadvantage   – Does not index journal articles.
                – Will not search by subject.

Subjects
best served   – Books and other materials published since 1970.

DATABASE SERVICES FOR INFORMATION ABOUT JOURNAL ARTICLES:

U-Search:

What   – You can learn to search any of over 80 databases in a variety of
                  subjects using the BRS After Dark search service. Ask at the
                  reference desk for further information.

How   – Monday through Thursday -- evenings, GMU faculty and students can
                  search a database for 15 minutes with the help of a librarian.   The
                  cost for students is $2.00; faculty are charged direct full costs.

Advantage   – You receive a printed list of sources immediately.

Disadvantage   – You do it yourself with guidance from a staff member.
                – Not all subjects are covered.

Subjects   – Sciences, technology, medicine, business, education and all social
best served   sciences.

Infotrac:

What   – A micro-computer based database of current events business and
                  general journals.

How   – Use the microcomputer at the reference desk any time. It's free.
                – Use the Library of Congress Subject Headings books to determine which
                  subject words are used.   Color coded function keys and a user
                  friendly menu driven system make it easy to use.

Advantage   – Produces a printed list of citations to journal articles on demand.
                – Anyone can use it.

Disadvantage   – Covers recent 4 years only.
                – Covers few scholarly journals.
Subjects
best served   – Business, current events and general social science.
Online Bibliographic Search Service:

George Mason University

What	– A librarian will search one of over 300 databases for GMU students or faculty using the Dialog, BRS, Wilsonline or Medline search services.
How	– Ask at the reference desk or call 323-2392 to set up an appointment with a librarian. $5.00 fee for students - full costs for faculty (may be charged to department's account).
Advantage	– A librarian will discuss your information needs and search strategy with you in depth. – A wide variety of subjects are covered in the databases. – Can answer more complex questions than Infotrac or U-Search.
Disadvantage	– Usually takes one week to get a printed list of sources.
Subjects best served	– Sciences, technology, business, education, all social sciences, and selected humanities disciplines.

* For information on how to use any of these services, stop by the reference desk or call 323-2392.

George Mason University

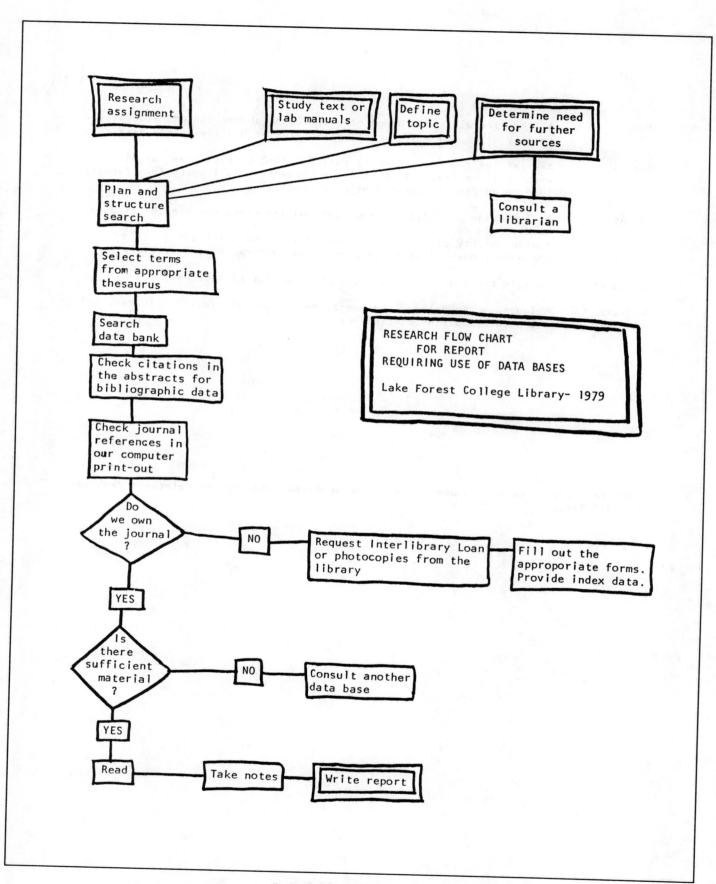

Research
assignment

Study text or
lab manuals

Define
topic

Determine need
for further
sources

Plan and
structure
search

Consult a
librarian

Select terms
from appropriate
thesaurus

RESEARCH FLOW CHART
FOR REPORT
REQUIRING USE OF DATA BASES

Lake Forest College Library- 1979

Search
data bank

Check citations in
the abstracts for
bibliographic data

Check journal
references in
our computer
print-out

Do
we own
the journal
?

NO

Request Interlibrary Loan
or photocopies from the
library

Fill out the
approporiate forms.
Provide index data.

YES

Is
there
sufficient
material
?

NO

Consult another
data base

YES

Read

Take notes

Write report

Lake Forest College

COMPUTERIZED LITERATURE SEARCHES

at the Los Alamos National Laboratory

WHEN YOU NEED

   ... A list of recent references on a particular topic.
   ... The papers published by a particular author in the last few years.
   ... Papers that reference a particular journal article.

WE CAN HELP!

A computerized or online literature search could satisfy these requests.

The library has access to over 200 databases or online indexes to the literature in the sciences, engineering, management, aerospace, energy technology, defense research, congressional hearings and more.

The databases can provide citations to journal articles, reports, books, conference papers, patents, theses, newspaper articles and other sources.

HOW CAN YOU GET A LITERATURE SEARCH?

Call the Reference Desk (7-5809) or come in person. You will be asked to fill out a Literature Search Request Form, giving a brief statement of your problem in a sentence or so, the time period to be searched, any relevant references on the topic, language restrictions for the search results, and any synonyms for terms in your request. The success of a search depends in large part on the accuracy and clarity of the request.

A preliminary search of an appropriate printed index may help you to define and describe your question. In addition, there are thesauri or lists of subject terms for many databases which may be consulted at the reference desk.

HOW LONG DOES IT TAKE?

Most searches are done in the order received, and the results are bibliographies that are printed offline at the database vendor's facility out of state. Offline prints are mailed to the Laboratory, which adds to the time elapsed from request to receipt of the results. Ordinarily, one should allow about ten days.

Only very simple requests such as an identification of an item or a brief list of an author's publications in one database may be done more quickly.

Los Alamos National Laboratory

WHAT IS THE OUTPUT?

You will receive a computer printout of bibliographic information on references
pertinent to your topic. The format of printouts varies with the systems and
databases searched. For some databases, abstracts can be included if you
request them.

WHAT ARE THE COSTS?

The library absorbs all costs of computerized literature searches at this time,
except for an occasional extensive search.

CAVEAT!

Computer databases generally cover the period from 1970 to the present. Earlier
material may be searched manually, which requires much more time than computer
searches.

Very general topics are not effectively searched by computer. Limitations on
temperature, pressure and speed of acceleration cannot be searched in most
data bases. Specific properties of well known substances or materials are
best found in handbooks.

OBTAINING THE MATERIAL THE SEARCH HAS IDENTIFIED

The library probably will not have in the collection all the citations found
by your search. To request those you wish to see, send the printout to
Mail Stop P362, with the desired references marked appropriately. Those in
the collection will be sent to you. You may order others by using the normal
library acquisition procedure of submitting a Libraries Material Request Form
for each desired item.

Los Alamos National Laboratory

SEARCH WORKSHEET
COMPUTER ASSISTED REFERENCE SERVICE

SEARCH NUMBER _____

SEARCH BY _____

SEARCH TOPICS:
. Describe the subject or topic you want researched, as completely as possible. List key
  words, terms, phrases or concepts that describe the topic. Give synonyms and any spelling
  variations. Also specify terms you do NOT want used in retrieving items.
      EXAMPLE: "Effect of any mutation on the eye colour of the fruit fly (Drosophila
                  melanogaster. *Not* wild."

_____

_____

_____

_____

_____

_____

_____

_____

_____

_____

_____

_____

_____

OTHER INFORMATION:

List two literature references, if known, which you have found useful on this topic; or
names of any researchers known to be working on the topic; dates or time periods relevant;
or any other related information.

_____

_____

_____

_____

DATA BASES TO BE SEARCHED:

_____

LANGUAGES WANTED: English only ▢   Any language ▢ Other (specify)_____

DATES: Range of years wanted (years of publication of cited items):

        All years available ▢   Not before 19____ . Other (specify)_____

About how many items do you expect may be found? _____   Do you want abstracts? Yes ▢ No ▢

DEADLINE: To be useful, this search must be completed by (date) _____

COST LIMIT: Give the approximate amount acceptable as a maximum cost. This will guide the
             searcher in selecting databases and determining scope of search. Queen's
             University Libraries will make every effort to honour that maximum but cannot
             guarantee to do so.

             Maximum cost $ _____

QUEEN'S UNIVERSITY AT KINGSTON
QUEEN'S UNIVERSITY LIBRARIES
COMPUTER ASSISTED REFERENCE SERVICE (CARS) -- SEARCH FORM
PINK COPY 4 -- ATTACH TO YELLOW COPY 2 & FILE BY SEARCH NUMBER

Queen's University at Kingston

"Computer Searching the Library"
U UNL 489/589
June 4 - 28, 1984
Instructors: S. Knapp; J. Gavryck

<u>Class Schedule</u>

SESSION	DATE/TIME	SUBJECT OF SESSION	FACULTY
1	Monday, June 4	Introduction; BRS demo; begin review of bibliographic network structure and citation structure	Gavryck Knapp
2	Tuesday, June 5	Searching for known item; Intro. to searching by subject; thesauri, ERIC and LCSH	Gavryck
3	Thursday, June 7	Introduction to online bib. structure and representation; LCS, OCLC, BRS ERIC, GEAC potential	Gavryck
4	Monday, June 11	The advent of the online card catalog; potential on- and off-site use	Gavryck Hudson
5	Tuesday, June 12	Introduction to database systems and searching	Knapp
6	Thursday, June 14	Boolean operators; thesauri	Knapp
7	Monday, June 18	Controlled vocabulary vs. free-text; Positional operators; limit capabilities - language population pub. date pub. type	Knapp
8	Tuesday, June 19	Planning search strategies; Subject heading searching; BRS "After Dark" practice	Knapp
9	Thursday, June 21	BRS "After Dark" Practice; exercises	Knapp Gavryck
10	Monday, June 25	BRS "After Dark" practice; exercises	Gavryck
11	Tuesday, June 26	"The Source" and "Electronic Bulletin Boards" demo	Burgess Gavryck
12	Thursday, June 28	"Knowledge Index" demo	Gavryck Knapp

SUNY-Albany

ADVANTAGES OF COMPUTER

LITERATURE SEARCHING

SPEED: One minute of computer searching is approximately equal to one hour of manual searching

CURRENCY: Databases are more up-to-date than printed sources

COVERAGE: Some databases include items not found in their printed equivalents

ACCESS: Computer searching provides a greater number of access points to information than printed sources

COST: Computer searching may be less "expensive" than manual searching

DISADVANTAGES OF COMPUTER

LITERATURE SEARCHING

SCOPE: Most databases cover the literature of only the past ten years or so

COVERAGE: Some topics do not have adequate online coverage

INTERMEDIARY: A librarian familiar with searching techniques is needed

COST: Computer searching may be more "expensive" than manual searching

University of California - Berkeley

ASK YOURSELF BEFORE YOU DO-IT-YOURSELF

1. Do I want my information online?

2. Is the information I want available online?

3. Do I want to retrieve the information myself?

4. Am I willing to make the following investments:
   a. access to/purchase of hardware
   b. access to/purchase of software
   c. start-up fee
   d. connect time fees (+ minimum monthly fee, if any)
   e. time and energy to acquire and maintain a new skill

   For the following returns:
   a. personal satisfaction
   b. convenience
   c. control
   d. speed?

5. Which vendor offers the package that best meets my needs?

6. All things considered, is my online alternative less or more attractive? My alternative is CRS: mediated searches on campus at near cost during regular business hours on an appointment basis run by an experienced searcher/information specialist with access to a greater range of databases.

University of California - Berkeley

NOT

Use of the NOT operator removes some element from the search. It rejects records that contain the term following the NOT.

```
?   SS   ENERGY NOT NUCLEAR

        7    6207    ENERGY
        8    2461    NUCLEAR
        9    5816    ENERGY NOT NUCLEAR
```

Of the 6207 records in set 7 which contain the word ENERGY, there are 5816 that do NOT contain the word NUCLEAR.

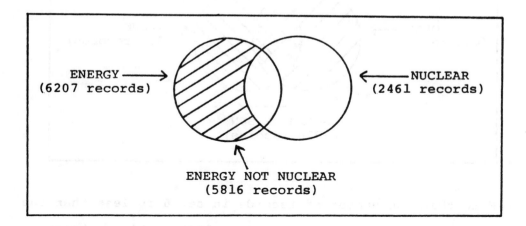

ENERGY ⟶ (6207 records)

⟵ NUCLEAR (2461 records)

ENERGY NOT NUCLEAR (5816 records)

The NOT operator is seldom used because one runs the risk of eliminating useful citations, e.g., a record entitled "Alternatives to Nuclear Energy" would be eliminated by the search strategy above.

University of California - Berkeley

OR

Use of the OR operator retrieves <u>all</u> records which
contain <u>any</u> of the ORed search terms.

```
?  SS   SOLAR OR SUN

        4    481    SOLAR
        5    302    SUN
        6    770    SOLAR OR SUN
```

Each of the 770 records retrieved in set 6 contains
<u>either</u> the word SUN OR the word SOLAR.

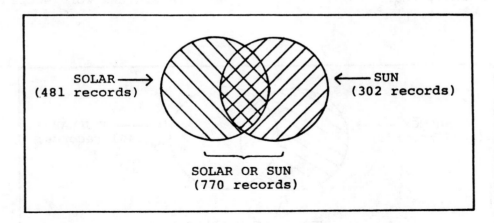

SOLAR ———➤   ◄——— SUN
(481 records)   (302 records)

SOLAR OR SUN
(770 records)

Note that the number of records in set 6 is less than the
sum of the two parts (481 + 302 ≠ 770). This is because
some of the records contain both the word SOLAR and the
word SUN, and are counted only once. In general, use of
the OR operator gives results greater than each of the parts.

University of California - Berkeley

BOOLEAN OPERATORS

There are three Boolean operators: AND, OR, NOT. The
operators are used to combine search terms into meaningful
relationships.

* * * * * * * * * *

AND

Use of the AND operator retrieves only those records which
contain all of the ANDed search terms.

```
? SS   SOLAR AND ENERGY

      1    481        SOLAR
      2   6207        ENERGY
      3    243        SOLAR AND ENERGY
```

Each of the 243 records retrieved in set 3 contains both
the word SOLAR AND the word ENERGY.

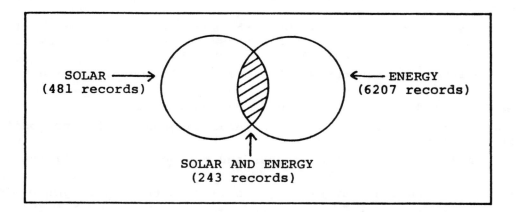

SOLAR ───▶   ◀─── ENERGY
(481 records)   (6207 records)

SOLAR AND ENERGY
(243 records)

Use of the AND operator almost always gives results
smaller than each of the parts.

University of California - Berkeley

COMPUTER LITERATURE SEARCHING CHECKLIST

1. Consult a librarian to determine the suitability of your topic for a computer literature search.

2. Set up an appointment; prior to your appointment, complete a CRS Search Request form using a database thesaurus if available.

3. During the presearch interview, you and the librarian:

    a. Identify the relevant database(s).

    b. Translate your keywords into search terms (descriptors and/or natural language) which are acceptable to the computer; consult a database thesaurus (if available) and database documentation.

    c. Connect your search terms into logical relationships using Boolean operators.

    d. Decide whether to print your citations online or offline.

    e. Decide which print format you prefer.

4. The librarian runs your search and you provide feedback; be prepared to modify your search strategy if something "unexpected" occurs.

5. Pay the cost recovery fee.

DO-IT-YOURSELF SEARCHING CHECKLIST

1. Identify the relevant database(s) by consulting your system user's manual.

2. If possible, consult a database thesaurus (many such thesauri are available at the Library); if a thesaurus is not available or convenient, use natural language search terms.

3. Connect your search terms into logical relationships using Boolean operators.

4. Wait until dark (or the weekend) to run your search.

5. Use descriptors found in your natural language "hits" to modify your search.

6. If something "unexpected" occurs and you need help, call the system customer service number.

7. Print or download your citations online in the format you prefer.

8. Pay the system at the end of the month.

University of California - Berkeley

GUIDE TO
SERVICES:

Do-it-Yourself
Computer Searching
with BRS/After Dark

What is it?	A User Friendly, Menu-Driven Computer Literature Search system you use yourself, offered at greatly reduced rates. It is available at night and on weekends.
What does it do?	The system scans indexes of journal articles or other literature and compiles a list of bibliographic citations (and abstracts) on the subject of your choice.
Who is eligible to use it?	UMO Faculty, Staff, Graduate Students, and anyone with a standing billing account with the Library.
When is it available?	Monday – Thursday, 6 p.m. to 9 p.m.; Saturday, 10 a.m. to 5 p.m.; and Sunday, 1 p.m. to 9 p.m.
How much does it cost?	$3.00 for 10 minutes, $6.00 for 20 minutes, $9.00 for a half hour – cost is based on time spent connected to the computer.
How do I pay?	The Library Business Office will bill you on a monthly basis.
What help will the Library provide?	The Library will provide basic instruction in use of the system (by appointment), basic instruction in search strategy formation (by appointment), use of the Library's IBM PC, use of the system instruction manual and manuals for various databases, and some coaching while you are online. The Library cannot provide basic instruction in use of the system or search strategy formation on demand, so talk to a Librarian before planning to search.
Who can I talk to for more help?	For more information, call the Information Services Desk at 581-1673 or the Science and Engineering Center at 581-1678.

RAYMOND H. FOGLER LIBRARY

University of Maine

ONLINE COMPUTERIZED SEARCHING OF BIBLIOGRAPHIC DATABASES

● **Van Pelt Library** ● **University of Pennsylvania**

1. WHAT IS "ONLINE SEARCHING"?

2. WHAT IS A DATABASE?

3. WHAT IS SEARCHABLE IN A DATABASE?

4. HOW CAN IT BE SEARCHED?

5. WHAT ARE THE ADVANTAGES AND CAPABILITIES OF COMPUTER SEARCHING?

6. WHAT SUBJECT AREAS ARE COVERED?

7. WHAT ARE THE SEARCH SERVICES OFFERED BY VAN PELT LIBRARY?

8. HOW IS A SEARCH ARRANGED?

1. WHAT IS "ONLINE SEARCHING"?

"Online searching" links our local terminal by telephone lines to a large
remote computer with which we can communicate and through which we can
request bibliographic citations and other information. We can access over
200 databases on several commerical systems: DIALOG in California, BRS in
New York, VU/TEXT in Philadelphia, QUESTEL in France, and others.

2. WHAT IS A DATABASE?

A bibliographic database is a set of citations, often with abstracts, to
books, articles, reports, etc., stored in machine-readable form. Some
databases, such as the Harvard Business Review Online on BRS or the
Philadelphia Inquirer on VU/TEXT contain the full text of the articles
they index.

Non-bibliographic databases provide statistics, scientific data, directory
information, news reports, reports on research in progress, etc.

Most of the databases which we search are the machine-readable online
equivalents of printed indexes. Frequently, the computer-stored
information that is used to produce the printed product forms the basis
for the online file. Some examples are: Psychological Abstracts, the
ERIC indexes, P.A.I.S., and Social Sciences Citation Index. In a few
cases up to 15 years or more of a file are searchable online; in most 10
years or less. In many files the citations include long abstracts.

University of Pennsylvania, Van Pelt Library

3.   WHAT IS SEARCHABLE IN A DATABASE?

Usually most of the information in a database is searchable: most words, phrases, codes, and numbers in each of its thousands of citations.

A typical citation includes: accession number (a number identifying the citation in the computer file, often the same number used in the printed index); author or authors; title; author's affiliation (sponsor or place of work); source (journal reference or book publisher); assigned subject headings (more on this below); an abstract or summary.

EXAMPLE CITATION:

Accession number	EJ279900 SE533270
Title	Is there Logo after Turtle Graphics?
Author	Lough, Tom; Tipps, Steve
Source	Classroom Computer News, v3 n5 p50-53 Spr 1983
Available from	Reprint UMI
Language	English
Document Type	Journal Article (080); Project Description (141)
Abstract	Ideas, suggestions, and program listings are provided to demonstrate Logo's list-processing capabilities. These include printing, writing, composing, and drawing words; word power, word lists, random words, and creating words. Program listings are for Apple (LCSI) Logo version. (JN)
Descriptors	*Computer Programs; Elementary Education; Learning Activites; *Microcomputers; *Programming; *Programming Languages; *Word Processing
Identifiers	List Processing; Logo Programming Language

Nearly everything in the above citation from the ERIC (education) database is searchable. Put another way: each citation is indexed by almost any and every word or number in it. Some of the searchable elements in this citation are:

    Title words: LOGO; TURTLE GRAPHICS

    Descriptors or Subject Terms: MICROCOMPUTERS; ELEMENTARY EDUCATION;
        PROGRAMMING LANGUAGES (A "descriptor" is an index word or phrase
        assinged to the citation by a human indexer, often from a formal
        controlled vocabulary. For many databases a published term list
        or a thesaurus aids in the selection of search terms.)

    Abstract: LIST PROCESSING; LOGO; APPLE; RANDOM WORDS; COMPOSING
        (These words and phrases are not title words or assigned index
        terms. They could not be directly searched in the printed
        Current Index to Journals in Education. They can be searched by
        computer.)

deolhand.doc

University of Pennsylvania, Van Pelt Library

4. HOW CAN IT BE SEARCHED?

A search term (a word, phrase, number, code, etc.) is typed into our terminal and sent to the computer. The computer responds with the number of citations indexed by this term (the number of "hits").

        We type: MICROCOMPUTERS

        The computer replies: (set#)   (no. of hits)   (term)
                                   1   1524   MICROCOMPUTERS

        We type: ELEMENTARY EDUCATION

        The computer replies: (set#)   (no. of hits)   (term)
                                   2   27424   ELEMENTARY EDUCATION

5. WHAT ARE THE ADVANTAGES AND CAPABILITIES OF COMPUTER SEARCHING?

Any number of search terms can be entered as above, each causing a set of citations to be created. If it is "index" terms which are entered, similar results could have been obtained manually by using a printed index, although possibly with more time and effort. Results are practically instantaneous online, and up to 15 years or more can be searched at once.

The chief advantage of computer searching, however, is its capability to do what cannot be done manually:

Searching "non-index" terms: words and phrases from titles and
    abstracts, especially new "buzzwords" which may be very specific and
    descriptive but are not yet used in printed indexes, may be searched
    online and are often effective search keys.

Combining concepts: logically combining sets of citations to produce
    another set, characterized by 2 or more terms or concepts at once, is
    the most powerful capability of computer searching:

    Example: We type: MICROCOMPUTERS AND ELEMENTARY EDUCATION

              Reply: 1   1524   MICROCOMPUTERS
                        2   27424   ELEMENTARY EDUCATION
                        3   86   1 AND 2

    Set number 3 contains just 86 citations, each of which is indexed by
    both of the desired index terms. These 86 citations could not have
    been isolated by manual methods, without scanning the thousands of
    citations under either index entry.

The Boolean operators "AND", "OR", and "NOT" control the logical relationships among sets. The "AND" operator denotes the "intersection" of two or more terms, and signifies that each term must be present in order for an item to be retrieved by the computer. This operator narrows the search results. The "OR" operator denotes the "union" of terms, and commands the computer to broaden the search, to retrieve items which

deolhand.doc

University of Pennsylvania, Van Pelt Library

contain any or all of the terms specified. The "NOT" operator signifies the "negation" of terms, and directs the computer to delete from the set to be retrieved those items which contain a certain term or terms. The combination process is often illustrated by Venn diagrams, as below:

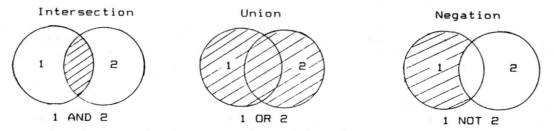

Intersection	Union	Negation
1 AND 2	1 OR 2	1 NOT 2

<u>Reviewing results</u>: During the actual performance of the search, sample citations, retrieved as a result of a particular search strategy, may be printed online at the computer terminal to determine the success of the search and to permit revision of the search strategy.

6.   WHAT SUBJECT AREAS ARE COVERED?

Most social science and humanities topics are searched at Van Pelt. Many departmental libraries do their own searching. Full descriptions of and subject indexes to the databases are available at the Van Pelt Reference Desk and in the appropriate departmental libraries listed below:

Biomedical	(898-5817)	Medicine, biology, nursing, health sciences
Chemistry	(898-5627)	Chemistry
Dental	(898-8969)	Dentistry
Engineering		
Moore	(898-8135)	Computer Science
Towne	(898-7266)	Engineering
Lippincott	(898-5924)	Business, management, applied economics
Math-Physics	(898-8173)	Mathematics, physics, astronomy
Museum	(898-7840)	Anthropology, archeology
Van Pelt	(898-7555)	Social sciences, humanities
Veterinary	(898-8874)	Veterinary medicine

7.   WHAT ARE THE SEARCH SERVICES OFFERED BY VAN PELT LIBRARY?

● DO YOUR OWN SEARCHES
   If you are a Penn student, faculty member or staff member, you can do your own search of the BRS/After Dark and DIALOG/Knowledge Index databases on our terminal. This service is available by appointment, several evenings a week and on weekends.

   Penn students also have the option of searching most BRS databases during the day, after attending the required training session.

deolhand.doc

The search cost is $4.00 for up to 30 minutes online, payable when you schedule your appointment. You may run 2 searches per week, up to a maximum of 10 per semester.

We suggest that you come to the Reference Desk and talk to a librarian ahead of time to discuss your topic, databases and search strategy. Assistance during your search is available at scheduled times or by appointment.

● SEARCH WITH A LIBRARIAN
Make a 1-hour appointment with an experienced searcher. You can review citations and modify your search strategy for better results. You can either have your citations printed online, without abstracts, at the time of the search, or offline, with abstracts, and sent to us in 4-7 working days. Over 200 databases are accessible through this service, from vendors such as BRS, Dialog, Questel and Vutext.

For Penn students, this service is subsidized, with some exceptions, for a cost to the user of $.35 per minute and $.15 per citation. A typical search costs $10-$15 dollars.

Penn faculty and staff are charged the full online connect time, type charges and/or offline print charges of the search, which vary from database to database.

Searches for patrons not affiliated with the University will be done at the discretion of the librarian. Users associated with an educational institution but who are not University of Pennsylvania faculty, staff, or students will be charged the full online and offline costs of the search and an additional $10 service fee. Commercial users will be charged the full online and offline costs of the search and an additional $30 service fee.

● HAVE SEARCHES DONE FOR YOU
You discuss your topic with a librarian who will later do your search. You should estimate the cost at $15 per database, although the actual costs will vary depending on the complexity of your topic and the databases you search. This service is available to Penn faculty, staff and students only.

8.   HOW IS A SEARCH ARRANGED?

To ask about a computer search, call the appropriate library. For a search in the social sciences or humanities, visit the Van Pelt Library Reference Desk or call 898-7555. A member of the Reference staff will discuss your topic with you to determine whether a database search could be useful and which type of search service will best meet your needs.

deolhand.doc

University of Pennsylvania, Van Pelt Library

COMPUTERIZED RESEARCH SERVICES IN VAN PELT LIBRARY

Van Pelt Library   **University of Pennsylvania**

Van Pelt Library offers a variety of computerized systems that can assist you in your research. This information sheet briefly describes the scope and availability of each system. Ask at Reference for more information.

Penn Libraries' holdings

There are several systems that you can search to find out if the Penn Libraries own a particular item and where that item is.

PennLIN (the Penn Libraries Information Network)
- bibliographic and location information for books, periodicals, newspapers
- items acquired or processed since 1972, in most Penn Libraries (for older materials, check the main card catalog)
- searchable by author, title, and Library of Congress or MeSH subject headings
- terminals available on the 1st floor in Van Pelt, and in departmental libraries
- dial-up access from personal computers, through PennNET
- Biblio, a software program available at Van Pelt Reference, will reformat a downloaded search into standard bibliographic form

Ordered or recently cataloged materials
- listed in the RLIN (Research Libraries Information Network) database
- a Librarian will search the RLIN terminal for you at the Reference Desk

Books currently charged out
- listed on small book location terminals located at the Circulation and Reserve desks and in the stacks
- shows circulation status for items in Van Pelt, Lippincott, Fine Arts libraries

National bibliographic networks

Van Pelt Reference can search two national bibliographic networks, which contain the cataloging and holdings information from thousands of libraries nationwide. With these systems we can verify citations and locate items.

RLIN (Research Libraries Information Network)
- contains holdings for 50 research and specialized libraries in U.S., including Temple, Princeton, Hopkins, Columbia, NYU, NYPL
- searchable by author, subject and title keyword
- also contains ESTC (18th-century English books), Avery (architectural periodicals), and Scipio (art catalogs) files

OCLC
- lists books and journals in more than 2500 U.S. libraries.
- local libraries include Drexel, Bryn Mawr, Haverford, Swarthmore, and the Free Library of Philadelphia
- searchable by author and title

University of Pennsylvania, Van Pelt Library

Indexing and abstracting services

These databases cite journal articles, and, in some cases, research reports, conference papers, dissertations, and books on a subject or by an author.

Available at no charge

CD ROM (compact disc systems)--**For Penn students, faculty and staff only**
-flexible and powerful searching using microcomputers
-available days, evenings, weekends, walk-in or by appointment
-assistance provided from Reference Desk
-databases: Psychological Abstracts, 1974-   Readers Guide, 1983-
ERIC (educational materials), 1966-   Humanities Index, 2/84-
Le Pac (U.S. documents), 1976-   Social Sciences Index, 4/83-

Available for a fee

Do-it-yourself searching--**For Penn students, faculty and staff only**
-you perform your own search on library terminals
-over 100 databases in the sciences, social sciences, and humanities are
        available through three end-user systems
-$4.00 for up to 30 minutes online
-assistance provided at regularly scheduled times, or by special appointment
-training offered regularly
-systems: BRS/After Dark--75 databases, available evenings and weekends
        Dialog/Knowledge Index--45 databases, available evenings and
            weekends
        BRS/Instructor--95 databases, available daytime, evenings and
            weekends, to trained students only

Searching-with-a-librarian
-over 400 databases in the sciences, social sciences, humanities on 5 systems
-a librarian does the search; you consult, modify search, review results
-appointments available Monday-Friday, 9-5
-Penn students are charged $.35/minute and $.15/citation
-Penn faculty/staff pay full online and offline costs (which vary by database)
-systems: BRS--115 databases
        Dialog--330 databases
        Vutext--Philadelphia Inquirer/Daily News (6 mins. free with Penn ID)
        Questel--the Francis databases, major European scholarly databases in
            the humanities and social sciences
        Wilsonline--24 databases corresponding to Wilson periodical indexes,
            covering a variety of disciplines

For more information, contact a librarian at Van Pelt Reference or in a departmental library.

BIOMEDICAL	898-5817	Medicine, biology, nursing, health sciences
CHEMISTRY	898-5627	Chemistry
DENTAL	898-8969	Dentistry
ENGINEERING		
MOORE	898-8135	Computer science
TOWNE	898-7266	Engineering
LIPPINCOTT	898-5924	Business, management, applied economics
MATH-PHYSICS	898-8173	Mathematics, physics, astronomy
MUSEUM	898-7840	Anthropology, archeology
VAN PELT	898-7555	Social sciences, humanities
VETERINARY	898-8874	Veterinary medicine

University of Pennsylvania, Van Pelt Library

Online Searching Guide:

Appendixes

**LIBRARY USERS AND ONLINE SYSTEMS:
SUGGESTED OBJECTIVES FOR
LIBRARY INSTRUCTION**

Prepared for the Direct Patron Access to Computer-Based Reference Systems Committee, Machine-Assisted Reference Section, Reference and Adult Services Division, American Library Association, January, 1985. Approved by the RASD Board of Directors, July 1985.

Dennis Hamilton

INTRODUCTION

The widespread use of personal computers in the home and in the office, combined with the increasing availability of various types of automated information systems in libraries, has opened up an important new area of user education. In libraries, many of these automated information systems are used directly and do not require the personal assistance of librarians as intermediaries between the library user and the information. Librarians want the users of these systems to be self-reliant and successful in accessing needed information. There is an expanding need to instruct library patrons who directly use online catalogs, online circulation systems, and other bibliographic and nonbibliographic databases. Librarians have a responsibility to develop instructional programs that will enable users to be successful with all types of online systems through the effective use of learned information access skills. During the 1982 Annual American Library Association Conference, the Direct Patron Access to Computer-Based Reference Systems Committee undertook a project to establish learning objectives for training direct users of computer-based information systems. The members of the committee compiled a bibliography of recent journal articles and books on the topic of end-user searching of online catalogs and vendor databases. Applying their professional expertise to this new area of library instruction, the committee members developed a draft of generic learning objectives for training searchers. Comments on the draft were solicited from the RASD membership by means of an announcement placed in *RASD Update*.

SCOPE AND PURPOSE

The objectives developed are designed to facilitate library instruction where any online system is used directly by patrons. They are intended for librarians who have responsibility for devising instructional programs for online systems in school, special, public, or academic libraries. These objectives provide an outline of general topics and skills to be covered in classroom or individual instruction. They may also be used by librarians who are seeking guidance for preparing printed or online instructional aids. A selected bibliography for further reading about online searching and the training of users follows the objectives.

INSTRUCTIONAL OBJECTIVES

1.   Understanding the system.
1.1.   The user will know which online systems are available and what each system represents.
1.1.1. The user will understand the relationships among the various online and manual systems provided by the library and will be able to choose the most appropriate system to satisfy a particular information need.
1.1.2. The user will be able to define the scope of each system in terms of the type of material included and the subjects and time or other periods covered, and will know which kinds of information are unique to a particular system.
1.1.3   The user will be aware of any fees incurred in using a particular system.

2.   Planning the search strategy.
2.1.   The user will be able to analyze each information need and to develop a search strategy appropriate to the need and the system.
2.1.1. The user will be able to identify the various files that are available in the system.
2.1.2. The user will know which access points may be used within a particular file to retrieve information.
2.1.3. The user will understand the syntax and function of Boolean operators and will be

able to use them to search the files in the system.
2.1.4. If the online system is under authority control, the user will understand the relationship between the authority file and other files in the system and will be able to identify and to use authoritative access points to search the system.
2.1.5. The user will understand the difference between free-text and controlled-vocabulary searching and will be able to determine which approach to use for the best search results.
2.1.6. The user will know how to select the search strategy that is the most efficient and uses the least amount of machine resources.
2.1.7. The user will understand how to narrow or broaden a search strategy.
2.1.8. The user will be aware of significant limitations of the online system.

3.   Operating the system.
3.1.   The user will be able to operate the system in an efficient manner.
3.1.1. The user will be able to operate the terminal and any auxiliary equipment or devices.
3.1.2. If necessary, the user will be able to log-on and log-off the system.
3.1.3. The user will be able to access the various files within the system.
3.1.4. The user will be able to enter search commands correctly.
3.1.5. If a choice is available, the user will be able to select the appropriate display format.
3.1.6. The user will be able to use the appropriate command(s) to page through a list of display results or to move forward or backward in the system.
3.1.7. The user will be able to comprehend and to respond appropriately to error messages and to other system prompts.
3.2.   The user will be able to obtain assistance in the use of the system.
3.2.1. The user will be aware of available online help commands and will be able to use them as needed.
3.2.2. The user will be aware of any available written aids or human resources that may be consulted for assistance.
3.2.3. The user will know when it is necessary or appropriate to refer a search to a search intermediary.

4.   Interpreting the search results.
4.1.   The user will understand how to interpret the search results and how to obtain the needed information.
4.1.1. The user will be able to identify the elements

of a search display and will be able to determine which elements are relevant in retrieving the needed information.

4.1.2. When more than one item of information is retrieved in the system, the user will understand the order in which items are displayed.

4.1.3. The user will understand any instructions or procedures necessary to obtain the information or the sources of information retrieved as a result of the search.

ONLINE TRAINING SESSIONS: SUGGESTED GUIDELINES

Developed by the Education and Training of Search Analysts Committee* of the Machine-Assisted Reference Section, Reference and Adult Services Division (RASD), American Library Association. Approved by the RASD Board of Directors, February 1981.

In planning an online training session it is important that both the trainer, whether a search service, database producer, or independent organization, and the host, whether a library, professional association, or online user's group, carefully plan and organize all aspects of such a program. Similarly, when search analysts or administrators consider whether to attend a session or attempt to evaluate the value of an attended session, it is important that they have some standard basis for comparison. The following guidelines are intended both to aid planners or trainers in preparing training sessions and to allow comparisons and evaluations of a given session.

Normal aspects of planning a workshop or training session (e.g., provision of refreshments or lunches, parking arrangements, restroom facilities, and so on) have not been included unless special arrangements are necessary. However, such guidelines must take into account the various types of online training sessions currently available. Therefore, these guidelines are presented for five types of training sessions: 1) Search Service--Beginning; 2) Search Service--Advanced; 3) Search

Service--Subject; 4) Database Producer; and 5) Independent Introductory Workshop.

A search service is defined as the system through which searchers gain access to particular databases. Examples include Systems Development Corporation (SDC), Bibliographic Retrieval Service (BRS), and Lockheed Information Service. Synonymous terms include vendors or search systems. Database producers compile and provide the individual databases to the search services. For example, the Educational Resources Information Center produces the ERIC database and then makes it available through various search services. They are also commonly referred to as database suppliers. Independent introductory workshops may be presented by individuals, libraries, library schools, or commercial information companies.

It is inadvisable, especially in these days of high inflation, to suggest a standard or even an appropriate fee range for the various types of training sessions. However, it should be remembered that the search services and database producers are selling a product, and a good, inexpensive presentation that attracts a large crowd promotes and increases use of their product. The fee charged, therefore, would be as low as possible. In no instance should a search service or database producer expect to gain a profit directly from the fees charged for any training session. Free training sessions, especially those of an introductory or beginning level, are to be encouraged.

Since cost is, however, a very important consideration, these guidelines utilize a sliding scale, from minimum to suggested to optimum, for most of the categories. "Minimum" represents the basic requirements for a successful training session and would be appropriate for a free or inexpensive session. If many of the "suggested" criteria are met for a given type of training session, increased fees would be appropriate. Similarly, sessions that are judged "optimum" in several categories could charge the highest fees.

---

*MARS Education and Training of Search Analysts Committee: Marilyn Cabonell, M. Virginia Jackson, Norene McDonald, Maureen Pastine, Carol Tobin, Becki Whitaker, Greg Byerly, Committee Chair.

ONLINE TRAINING SESSIONS: SUGGESTED GUIDELINES

	SEARCH SERVICE: BEGINNING TRAINING	SEARCH SERVICE: ADVANCED TRAINING	SEARCH SERVICE: SUBJECT TRAINING	DATABASE PRODUCER TRAINING	INTRODUCTORY WORKSHOP (INDEPENDENT)
PURPOSE	To introduce searching concepts and procedures in a specific system. The session will deal almost entirely with searching the given vendor's databases.	To refine searching techniques in a specific system. The session will deal only with searching in the given vendor's system.	To refine skills for multiple database searching in subject-related files in a specific system. The sessions will deal only with searching in the given vendor's system.	To provide a basic understanding of the construction and searching capabilities in specific databases without regard to systems used. The session will use one or more vendor's systems.	To introduce and explain the basic concepts of computer searching and to show its applications in library reference work. One or more vendor's systems may be demonstrated.
AUDIENCE LEVEL	New searchers, minimal online experience. First training session or first training in this system. OPTIMUM: Designed for *either* new searchers *or* experienced searchers new to this specific system.	Experienced searcher, experienced in a specific system. PREREQUISITE: System's beginning training or appropriate in-house training on the system. OPTIMUM: 10 hours of online experience in the system	Experienced searcher, experienced in the specific system. PREREQUISITE: System's beginning training or appropriate in-house training on the system. MINIMUM: Some degree of subject knowledge in the areas to be demonstrated. OPTIMUM: 10 hours of online experience in the system	Experienced searcher in at least one system. Some degree of subject knowledge in the areas to be demonstrated	No online experience or previous exposure
AUDIENCE SIZE	MINIMUM: No more than 30 people. SUGGESTED: One trainer for each 10–15 people	MINIMUM: No more than 25 people. SUGGESTED: 10–15 people	MINIMUM: No more than 25 people. SUGGESTED: 10–15 people. OPTIMUM: One trainer for each 5–10 people	MINIMUM: No more than 25 people. SUGGESTED: 15–20 people. OPTIMUM: One trainer for each 10–12 people	MINIMUM: No more than 50 people. SUGGESTED: No more than 30 people
LENGTH OF SESSION	MINIMUM: 1 day (6–8 hours). SUGGESTED: 2 days (12–16 hours)	MINIMUM: ½ day (4 hours). SUGGESTED: 1 day (6–8 hours)	MINIMUM: ½ day (4 hours). SUGGESTED: 1 day (6–8 hours)	MINIMUM: ½ day (4 hours). SUGGESTED: 1 day (6–8 hours)	MINIMUM: ½ day (4 hours). OPTIMUM: 1 day (6–8 hours)
TRAINER'S EXPERIENCE	MINIMUM: Systems expert. SUGGESTED: Generalist (generally familiar with all databases in system). OPTIMUM: Library experience	MINIMUM: Systems expert. SUGGESTED: Generalist (generally familiar with all databases in system). OPTIMUM: Library experience	MINIMUM: Experienced searcher with both appropriate subject specialization and system expertise. SUGGESTED: Generalist (could use local resource person). OPTIMUM: Library experience in the subject area to be demonstrated	MINIMUM: Experienced searcher with appropriate subject expertise. SUGGESTED: Generalists (generally familiar with all databases on all systems (could use local resource person). OPTIMUM: Library experience in the subject area to be demonstrated	MINIMUM: Experienced searcher with library experience. SUGGESTED: Generalists (generally familiar with all databases and various systems; could utilize local resource person)
TERMINALS AND PHONES	MINIMUM: 1 terminal, 1 phone (outside line). SUGGESTED: 1 terminal for every 3–4 people. OPTIMUM: DIGI-LOG-type terminal	MINIMUM: 1 terminal, 1 phone (outside line). SUGGESTED: 1 terminal for every 4–5 people. OPTIMUM: DIGI-LOG-type terminal	MINIMUM: 1 terminal, 1 phone (outside line). SUGGESTED: 1 terminal for every 4–5 people	MINIMUM: 1 terminal, 1 phone (outside line). SUGGESTED: 1 terminal for every 4–5 people	MINIMUM: 1 terminal, 1 phone (outside line). SUGGESTED: DIGI-LOG-type terminal
EQUIPMENT	MINIMUM: Blackboard or flip chart. SUGGESTED: Overhead projector or slide projector, as requested by trainer. OPTIMUM: DIGI-LOG-type terminal and monitors	MINIMUM: Blackboard or flip chart. SUGGESTED: Overhead projector or slide projector, as requested by trainer. OPTIMUM: DIGI-LOG-type terminal and monitors	MINIMUM: Blackboard or flip chart. SUGGESTED: Overhead projector or slide projector, as requested by trainer. OPTIMUM: DIGI-LOG-type terminal and monitors	MINIMUM: Blackboard or flip chart. SUGGESTED: Overhead projector or slide projector, as requested by trainer. OPTIMUM: DIGI-LOG-type terminal and monitors	MINIMUM: Blackboard or flip chart. SUGGESTED: Overhead projector or slide projector, as requested by trainer. OPTIMUM: DIGI-LOG-type terminal and monitors
HANDOUTS	MINIMUM: General information sheet listing name of the trainer, phone number, etc. Print versions of all transparencies. General descriptive outline of points to be covered. SUGGESTED: Workbook or descriptive guide with examples, exercises, etc. List of available search aids, manuals, etc. OPTIMUM: Advance distribution of appropriate handouts	MINIMUM: General information sheet listing name of the trainer, phone number, etc. Print versions of all transparencies. General descriptive outline of points to be covered. SUGGESTED: Workbook or descriptive guide with examples, exercises, etc. List of available search aids, manuals, etc. OPTIMUM: Advance distribution of appropriate handouts	MINIMUM: General information sheet listing name of the trainer, phone number, etc. Print versions of all transparencies. General descriptive outline of points to be covered. SUGGESTED: Workbook or descriptive guide with examples, exercises, etc. Subject-specialized list of all appropriate manuals, search aids, newsletters, etc. OPTIMUM: Advance distribution of appropriate handouts	MINIMUM: General information sheet listing name of the trainer, phone number, etc. Print versions of all transparencies. General descriptive outline of points to be covered. SUGGESTED: Workbook or descriptive guide with examples, exercises, etc. Subject-specialized list of all appropriate manuals, search aids, etc. OPTIMUM: Advance distribution of appropriate handouts	MINIMUM: General information sheet listing name of the trainer, phone number, etc. Print versions of all transparencies. General descriptive outline of points to be covered. SUGGESTED: Promotional handouts from the various search systems

ONLINE TRAINING SESSIONS: SUGGESTED GUIDELINES (cont.)

	SEARCH SERVICE: BEGINNING TRAINING	SEARCH SERVICE: ADVANCED TRAINING	SEARCH SERVICE: SUBJECT TRAINING	DATABASE PRODUCER TRAINING	INTRODUCTORY WORKSHOP (INDEPENDENT)
RESOURCES	MINIMUM: Vendor manual and examples of thesauri and aids Examples of appropriate printed indexes SUGGESTED: Enough manuals and aids for individual or group use	MINIMUM: Vendor manual and examples of thesauri and aids SUGGESTED: Enough manuals and aids for individual or small group use	MINIMUM: Vendor manual and examples of thesauri and aids Examples of appropriate printed indexes SUGGESTED: Enough manuals and aids for individual or group use	MINIMUM: Major search aids of databases to be demonstrated Examples of appropriate printed indexes SUGGESTED: Examples of search aids, thesauri, newsletters, etc., for each database to be demonstrated Enough manuals and aids for individual or group use	MINIMUM: Display of sample manuals, search aids, and thesauri Examples of appropriate printed indexes
ONLINE TIME DEMONSTRATION	MINIMUM: Terminal available for online demonstrations as needed SUGGESTED: Online demonstrations of various procedures, i.e. logging on, etc.	MINIMUM: Terminal available for online demonstrations, as needed SUGGESTED: Online explanation of problems or confusing commands, as requested by the audience OPTIMUM: Online resolution of problem searches brought by the audience, by advance request	MINIMUM: Terminal available for online demonstrations, as needed SUGGESTED: Online comparison of databases' coverage of similar topics OPTIMUM: Online resolution of problem searches brought by the audience, by advance request	MINIMUM: Terminal available for online demonstrations as needed SUGGESTED: Online comparison of how different systems handle the same database OPTIMUM: Online resolution of problem searches brought by the audience, by advance request	MINIMUM: Online demonstrations of various procedures SUGGESTED: Online searching of topics suggested by the audience
ONLINE TIME, INDIVIDUAL	MINIMUM: ½ hour structured, individual online time SUGGESTED: ½-1 hour, both structured and unstructured online time	MINIMUM: None: optional SUGGESTED: Structured or unstructured online practice, possibly in small groups	MINIMUM: None: optional SUGGESTED: Structured or unstructured online practice, possibly in small groups	MINIMUM: None: optional SUGGESTED: Structured or unstructured online time, possibly in small groups	MINIMUM: None: optional
ONLINE TIME, POSTSESSION	MINIMUM: None: optional SUGGESTED: 1-2 hours, either structured or unstructured, with possibility of help by phone	MINIMUM: None: optional SUGGESTED: ½-1 hour, either structured or unstructured, with possibility of help by phone	MINIMUM: None: optional SUGGESTED: ½ hour per database, up to 1 hour, with the possibility of help by phone	MINIMUM: None: optional SUGGESTED: ½ hour per database, up to 1 hour, with the possibility of help by phone	MINIMUM: None: optional
TYPE OF PRESENTATION	Lecture format with online demonstrations	Lecture/question-and-answer format	Lecture/question-and-answer format	Lecture/question-and-answer format	Lecture format with online demonstrations
REGISTRATION AND PUBLICITY	MINIMUM: Required advance registration Publicity should clearly state audience level, cost, length, etc. SUGGESTED: Identify backgrounds of audience, before the session, if possible	MINIMUM: Required advance registration Publicity should clearly state subject and databases to be covered SUGGESTED: Allow prior input concerning areas of problems or confusion OPTIMUM: Advance distribution of worksheets and/or free prior online time	MINIMUM: Required advance registration Publicity should clearly state subject and search systems to be covered SUGGESTED: Allow prior input concerning areas of confusion or problems OPTIMUM: Advance distribution of worksheets and/or free prior online time	MINIMUM: Required advance registration Publicity should clearly state audience level, cost, length, etc.	MINIMUM: Required advance registration Publicity should clearly state audience level, cost, length, etc.
LOCATION AND FACILITY	MINIMUM: Adequately sized room, with telephone SUGGESTED: Adjacent facility with additional terminals and phones OPTIMUM: Easily accessible by public transportation	MINIMUM: Adequately sized room, with telephone SUGGESTED: Adjacent facility with additional terminals and phones OPTIMUM: Easily accessible by public transportation	MINIMUM: Adequately sized room, with telephone SUGGESTED: Adjacent facility with additional terminals and phones OPTIMUM: Easily accessible by public transportation	MINIMUM: Adequately sized room, with telephone SUGGESTED: Adjacent facility with additional terminals and phones OPTIMUM: Easily accessible by public transportation	MINIMUM: Adequately sized room, with telephone SUGGESTED: Easily accessible by public transportation
EVALUATION	MINIMUM: Complete evaluation form at end of session SUGGESTED: Distribution of results to host	MINIMUM: Complete evaluation form at end of session SUGGESTED: Distribution of results to host	MINIMUM: Complete evaluation form at end of session SUGGESTED: Distribution of results to host	MINIMUM: Complete evaluation form at end of session SUGGESTED: Distribution of results to host	MINIMUM: Complete evaluation form at the end of the session
FOLLOW-UP BY TRAINER	SUGGESTED: Provide individual follow-up by mail or phone	SUGGESTED: Provide individual follow-up by mail or phone	SUGGESTED: Provide individual follow-up by mail or phone	SUGGESTED: Provide individual follow-up by mail or phone	SUGGESTED: Provide names, addresses, and phone numbers of appropriate contact persons

Online Searching Guides:
Bibliographies

Library Orientation and Instruction--1985

Hannelore B. Rader

The following is an annotated list of materials dealing with library orientation to facilities and services, instruction in the use of information resources, and computer skills related to information gathering. This is *RSR*'s 12th annual review of this particular literature and covers items published in 1985. A few references are not annotated because the compiler could not obtain a copy of them for the review.

Included in the list are publications on user instruction in all types of libraries and for all types of users, from small children to senior citizens. No publication in a foreign language is included. The items are arranged by type of library, and within that, alphabetically by author or title if there is not author.

In 1985, there was a substantial decrease in publications related to user instruction--47 percent as follows:

academic libraries	56 percent
public libraries	no entries
school libraries	9 percent
special libraries	38 percent
all types	34 percent

It is unclear at this time why the number of publications decreased at such a high rate, the highest decrease since this annual review began in 1973. There was only one other decrease previously-- a 15 percent decrease in 1982.

It must be noted that, as usual, the largest number of publications are related to user instruction in academic libraries, which also had the largest decrease (56 percent). The second highest number

Rader is director of University Libraries at Cleveland State University, Cleveland, Ohio.

of publications are concerned with library skills instruction in school libraries, where a 9 percent decrease occurred. The next highest number of publications deal with user instruction on all levels and indicates a 34 percent decrease. The lowest number of entries are concerned with user instruction in special libraries where a 38 percent decrease can be noted. There were no items related to user instruction in public libraries.

Again this year, it must be pointed out that an increasing number of publications deal with theoretical frameworks of and research related to bibliographic instruction and appear in library as well as discipline-oriented journals. This trend is likely to continue as librarians build closer liaisons with other professionals and their associations.

Other observations can also be noted:

- The trend of writing about the place of microcomputers in user instruction is continuing.
- An increasing number of publications deal with training end-users and teaching the use of online catalogs.
- School librarians are becoming more active in curriculum development and are planning and implementing programs that are course-integrated.
- Several articles address user instruction for international students.
- There is an increase in the number of regional and local workshops addressing user instruction.
- Computer-assisted programs on microcomputers to teach information skills in an academic setting are beginning to be published.

ACADEMIC LIBRARIES

Adams, Mignon S. and J.H. Morris. *Teaching Library Skills for Academic Credit*. Phoenix: Oryx Press, 1985.

This is a guide for the development and maintenance of a library course. It provides political strategies in instituting such a course and teaching methodology. The guide also gives course descriptions of such sources offered in various parts of the country.

Alfors, Inez L. and M.H. Loe. "Foremothers and Forefathers: One Way to Preserve and Enhance the Library Research Paper." *Research Strategies* 3 (Winter 1985): 4-16.

This paper describes a library instruction unit in a freshman composition course, which is based on biography topics to enhance instruction. Actual worksheets are included.

Arnott, Patricia and D.E. Richards. "Using the IBM Personal Computer for Library Instruction." *Reference Services Review* 13 (Spring 1985): 69-72.

Describes the University of Delaware Library instruction program based on computer-assisted instruction using IBM-PCs.

Bailey, Bill. "Thesis Practicum and the Librarian's Role." *Journal of Academic Librarianship* 11 (May 1985): 79-81.

The author suggests a formal thesis practicum program in the library conducted by a librarian on an one-to-one basis to help students be more efficient in preparing their theses.

Bain, Nancy R. and G.W. Bain. "Teaching Library Resources in Geography." *Journal of Geography* 84 (May-June 1985): 126-128.

This article describes a library instruction geography workbook for upper level college students and graduates.

Bergen, Kathleen and B. MacAdam. "One-on-One: Term Paper Assistance Programs." *College and Research Libraries* 46 (Spring 1985): 333-340.

The authors discuss motivating factors and a statistical analysis of user characteristics related to term paper assistance programs in academic libraries with special emphasis on the University of Michigan program.

Bhullar, Pushpajit. "LUMIN User Education." *Show-Me-Libraries* 36 (August 1985): 13-18.

LUMIN (Libraries of the University of Missouri Information Network) user education program is described including workshops, brochures, tours, course-related instruction, and a credit course to teach online catalog use.

Blazek, Ron. "Effective Bibliographic Instruction Programs: A Comparison of Coordinators and Reference Heads in ARL Libraries." *RQ* 24 (Summer 1985): 433-441.

Blazek reports findings of a survey of research libraries that examined the relationship between middle managers and bibliographic instruction programs. He makes recommendations regarding the value of the instructional coordinator in large academic libraries.

Bopp, Richard E. and S.J. VanDerLaan. "Finding Statistical Data." *Research Strategies* 3 (Spring 1985): 81-86.

The authors present a search strategy for locating published statistical data, which can be used by undergraduates. They provide a flow chart and suggest additional applications for this search strategy.

Cage, Alvin D. "User Education." *Texas Library Journal* 61 (Spring 1985): 8,10.

Cage describes the comprehensive library instruction program at Stephen F. Austin State University in Texas where the library is a full partner in the educational enterprise.

Chiang, Katherine S. and B. Kautz. "The Malti's Chicken: A Different Kind of Video." *Research Strategies* 3 (Summer 1985): 143-146.

This article discusses the effectiveness of a humorous videotape in bibliographic instruction and the possibility of producing such a film with a low budget and limited time based on the University of Minnesota experience.

Cope, Johnnye and E. Black. "New Library Orientation for International Students." *College Teaching* 33 (Fall 1985): 159-162.

The authors describe a special library instruction program for international students developed at North Texas State University at Denton based on their cultural differences.

Courtois, Martin, et al. *UIC Research Manual: Everything You Didn't Necessarily Want to Know about Writing Research Papers, but Need to Find Out.* ERIC Reproduction Service, 1985. ED 255 941.

This work presents the handbook used at the University of Illinois at Chicago to teach basic research paper skills in English composition classes.

Crittenden, William F. and V.L. Crittenden. "What's a Bibliography?" *Journal of Business Education* 60 (January 1985): 150-152.

The Crittendens discuss the need for library skills instruction in introductory business courses.

Davidson, Nancy M. "Innovative Bibliographic Instruction: Developing Outreach Programs in an Academic Library." *South Carolina Librarian* 29 (Spring 1985): 19-20.

Davidson describes several outreach library instruction programs at Winthrop College, in South Carolina, involving high school students in an advanced placement program, prospective freshmen, and an academic development program for gifted fifth and sixth graders.

Debreczeny, Gillian. "Coping with Numbers: Undergraduates and Individualized Term Paper Consultations." *Research Strategies* 3 (Fall 1985): 156-163.

Debreczeny discusses term paper clinics as an effective method of bibliographic instruction at the University of North Carolina. Practical methods for further improvement are provided.

Dodd, Jane, et al. *Texas A&M University Library. A Final Report from the Public Services Research Project. A Comparison of Two End User Operated Search Systems. One of a Series of Self Studies and Research Projects.* ERIC Reproduction Service, 1985. ED 255 224.

The authors summarize research involving the impact of end-user searching on library staff and users. BRS/After Dark and Search Helper were used in this assessment.

"Earlham College Still a Model for Course Integrated BI." *College and Research Libraries News* 46 (June 1985): 295.

This article describes Earlham College's bibliographic instruction program briefly with special focus on their bibliographic instruction workshop.

Engeldinger, Eugene A. "A Bibliographic Instruction for Study Abroad Programs." *College and Research Libraries News* 46 (September 1985): 395-398.

An American academic librarian tells of his experiences relating to bibliographic instruction in Japan both for Japanese and exchange students. A number of suggestions are provided to prepare students for educational exchanges particularly as related to BI.

Fairhall, Donald. "In Search of Searching Skills." *Journal of Information Science* 10 (1985): 111-123.

Fairhall defines a set of skills needed to search subject indexes. He presents a study of 129 students in the Ballarat College of Advanced Education in Australia majoring in library-science and psychology to measure their searching skills. The field is studied to establish the predictive validity of the processing skills students.

Friend, Linda. "Independence at the Terminal: Training Student End Users to Do Online Literature Searching." *Journal of Academic Librarianship* 11 (July 1985): 136-141.

Friend describes an end-user training program developed at Pennsylvania State University to teach BRS/After Dark.

Fryman, James F. and P.J. Wilkenson. "Federal Statistics: Teaching the Basics to Geography Students." *Journal of Geography* 84 (May-June 1985): 128-130.

The authors describe teaching methods used by faculty and librarians at the University of Northern Iowa to teach geography students how to locate U.S. government statistics.

Gratch, Bonnie. "Toward a Methodology for Evaluating Research Paper Bibliographies." *Research Strategies* 3 (Fall 1985): 170-177.

Gratch discusses criteria and processes for evaluating student bibliographies. She offers specific recommendations regarding selection of samples, hypotheses, and rating of bibliographies.

Hansen, Forest and J.H. Lee. "Ancient Greek History as a Library Instruction Course." *Research Strategies* 3 (Spring 1985): 65-74.

The authors describe a library research course in ancient Greek civilization taught cooperatively by a faculty member and a librarian at Lake Forest College in Illinois.

Hanson, Janet R. "Teaching Information Sources in Business Studies: An Application of the Theories of J. Bruner and R.M. Gagne." *Journal of Librarianship* 17 (July 1985): 185-199.

The author advocates the use of Bruner's and Gagne's educational theories in planning user instruction programs with special applications to business studies in an academic setting.

Hilton, Anne. "Guiding for Induction in a Polytechnic Library." *Infuse* 9 (April 1985): 7-12.

Hilton discusses a theoretical framework for user instruction, especially orientation and basic library skills for beginning college students. She provides guidelines and criteria for effective guides.

Hutson, Mary M. and W. Parson. "A Model of Librarianship for Combining Learning and Teaching." *Research Strategies* 3 (Spring 1985): 75-80.

The authors describe Evergreen State College's revised bibliographic instruction program, which is based on librarians' expertise in information handling, as well as their familarity with the substance of intellectual products.

Jarvis, William E. "Integrating Subject Pathfinders into Online Catalogs." *Database* (February 1985): 65-67.

Jarvis discusses integrating pathfinders for users into online catalogs to facilitate the teaching and learning of search strategies. Samples are provided.

Johnson, Hilary and M. Fisk. "Basic Library Orientation Using the Edfax Package." *Infuse* 9 (August 1985): 5-7.

Johnson and Fisk explain the use of microcomputers and video technology to orient freshmen to Plymouth Polytechnic's learning resource center in Great Britain.

Kendrick, Aubrey W. "BI for Business Students." *College and Research Libraries News* 46 (October 1985): 482-482,486.

Kendrick reports on the experience of teamteaching a required bibliographic instruction course for business students at the University of Alabama. He also provides the course outline.

Kenney, Donald and L. Wilson. "Education for the Online Access Catalog: A Model." *Research Strategies* 3 (Fall 1985): 164-169.

The authors present the various components of a model user education program for an outline catalog and its integration in the total existing bibliographic instruction program at Virginia Polytechnic Institute and State University.

Kirkendall, Carolyn. "Many Questions, Many Comments...and More Needed." *Research Strategies* 3 (Fall 1985): 191-193.

In this column, instruction librarians comment on the relationship between successful BI programs and the absence of internal conflict in the library, foreign students, and online searching.

_____. *Marketing Instructional Services: Applying Private Sector Techniques to Plan and Promote Bibliographic Instruction.* Ann Arbor, MI: Pierian Press, 1986.

This volume presents all the papers presented at the 13th Library Instruction Conference held at Eastern Michigan University, 3-4 May 1984. Included are "Marketing for Libraries" by Elizabeth Wood; "Marketing Beyond Our Means: The Ecological Consequences of Outreach" by William Miller; Virginia Tiefel's "Marketing Bibliographic Instruction in a Large University: The Seller's View;" Goodwin Berguist's "The Buyer's View"; "Promoting User Education: The British Perspective" by Ian Malley; Paula Warnken's "Designing and Promoting the 'Right' BI Program: A Holistic Approach;" and Peggy Berber's "Ten Things I Have Learned about Public Relations." In addition, it contains abstracts of seven poster sessions related to marketing BI, two bibliographies, and copies of handouts.

_____. "The Online Catalog or...You Can Lead a Horse to Water but You Can't Make It Search." *Research Strategies* 3 (Summer 1985): 140-142.

Kirkendall addresses issues related to the online catalog such as its use and appropriate search strategies, evolution of information, and the role of the reference librarian. She also discusses enduser searching.

_____. "Online Reference Services' Impact on Bibliographic Instruction." *Research Strategies* 3 (Winter 1985): 40-43.

Questions concerning who should be taught online searching, when, and how, and who should pay for this are addressed by several librarians. Bibliographic instruction for foreign students is also addressed.

_____. "To Teach Manual or Online Searching?" *Research Strategies* 3 (Spring 1985): 93-95.

Kirkendall presents reactions to the information equity problem related to online searching as well as the proper timing of bibliographic instruction.

Krieger, Tillie. "What the Traveling Scholar Needs to Know: An Opinion Piece." *Research Strategies* 3 (Summer 1985): 131-134.

Krieger provides several strategies for librarians and traveling scholars to cooperate in helping the scholars use libraries more effectively.

Larson, Inez A. and M.J. Loe. "Foremothers and Forefathers: One Way to Preserve and Enhance the Library Research Paper." *Research Strategies* 3 (Winter 1985): 4-16.

The authors discuss problems with freshmen research papers and how a library research unit based on biography can be an effective library instruction project. An outline for the unit is given.

Larson, Mary E. and Dace Freivalds. *Pennsylvania State University Libraries. A Final Report from the Public Services Research Projects. The Effect of an Instruction Program on Online Catalog Users. One of a Series of Self Studies and Research Projects.* ERIC Reproduction Service, 1985. ED 255 223.

This study examines three relationships to evaluate the effects of an instructional program on the online catalog use: the methods used to teach the use of the catalog, user reactions to the online catalog, search accuracy, and time-related efficiency.

Lubans, John, Jr. "Library Literacy." *RQ* 25 (Winter 1985): 191-194.

Carson Holloway, from the University of North Carolina at Chapel Hill, discusses user instruction related to the online catalog and relevant planning for it.

_____. "Library Literacy." *RQ* 24 (Spring 1985): 255-258.

This column presents Girja Kumar's view of library instruction. Kumar is the president of the Indian Library Association and librarian at Jawaharlal Nehru University in India. His philosophical reason for user education is to enable the user to find and use information independently.

MacAdam, Barbara. "Humor in the Classroom: Implications for the Bibliographic Instruction Librarian." *College and Research Libraries* 46 (July 1985): 327-333.

MacAdam examines the influence of the personal teaching style of instruction librarians in the classroom situation. Special attention is paid to using humor in bibliographic instruction and caution is advised.

Madland, Denise. "Library Instruction for Graduate Students." *College Teaching* 33 (Fall 1985): 163-164.

Madland discusses the library instruction needs of graduate students and describes a special program for them at the University of Wisconsin-Stout.

Malley, Ian. "User Education." In *College Librarianship*, edited by A. Rennie McElroy, 271-284. London: Library Association, 1984.

Malley provides an overview of user education in tertiary education in the United Kingdom. He discusses orientation and instruction in college and polytechnic libraries.

McCarthy, Constance. "The Faculty Problem." *Journal of Academic Librarianship* 11 (July 1985): 142-145.

The author discusses faculty-librarian cooperation for bibliographic instruction and faculty's lack of preparation in library research skills teaching.

McNeer, Elizabeth J. "Administrator's Perspective on Library Instruction." *Journal of Library Administration* 6 (Spring 1985): 65-69.

The purpose of the paper is to present a view of bibliographic instruction programs as a component of the continued growth and health of the total academic institution. McNeer discusses strategies for integrating faculty and librarians.

McQuistion, Virginia F. "What is Not on the Card Matters Too: A Follow-Up to 'Information on Cards and What It Means.'" *Research Strategies* 3 (Winter 1985): 44-45.

McQuistion describes an exercise used at Millikin University to teach students information not in the card catalog such as plays, poems, and essays.

Mech, Terrence. *Library Skills for Teachers: A Self-Paced Workbook.* ERIC Reproduction Service, 1985. ED 261 689.

Mech provides a self-paced workbook to introduce education students to basic library resources in their field. The workbook includes assignments and self-tests.

Miller, Constance and J. Rettig. "Reference Obsolence." *RQ* 25 (Fall 1985): 52-58.

Miller and Rettig compare practices and theories of a current academic library reference service with that of the nineteenth century and Samuel Gran's theory. They discuss user instruction as part of reference service.

Nahl-Jakobovits, Diane and L.A. Jakobovits. "Managing the Affective Micro-Information Environment." *Research Strategies* 3 (Winter 1985): 17-28.

The authors discuss several principles affecting motivational levels of users of information services, particularly, as related to the micro-information environment.

Neilsen, Mary Ann and M. Bremner. "Computer Assisted Instruction in the Australian National University Library." *Infuse* 9 (April 1985): 12-15.

The authors describe a CAI program developed at the Australian National University to teach students library and catalog using Apple II+ microcomputers. Included are modules on library services, using the catalog, and how to research a topic.

Nielson, Brian, et al. *Educating the Online Catalog User: A Model for Instructional Development and Education. Final Report. Revised.* ERIC Reproduction Service, 1985. ED 261 679.

The authors describe a model online catalog instructional system developed by three academic libraries.

Parsch, Janet. "Bibliographic Instruction: A Common Sense Approach." *Arkansas Libraries* 42 (June 1985): 6-10.

Patrick, R. "Learning-to-Learn-Skills--an Alternative to Traditional Library Skills." *Arkansas Libraries* 42 (June 1985): 12-14.

Ramey, Mary Ann. "Learning to Think about Libraries: Focusing and Attitudinal Change for Remedial Studies Students." *Research Strategies* 3 (Summer 1985): 125-130.

Ramey describes a bibliographic instruction program for developmental students. Emphasis is on encouraging students to think actively by using partners for discussions and flexibility.

Ridgeway, Trish. "Planning and Designing Library Floorplans." *Research Strategies* 3 (Summer 1985): 135-139.

Ridgeway provides guidelines for librarians to design floorplans of their facilities.

Sayles, Jeremy W. "Course Information Analysis: Foundation for Creative Library Support." *Journal of Academic Librarianship* 10 (January 1985): 343-345.

The author discusses librarians' role in course descriptions and syllabi analyses to provide better guides and instructional services. He provides details on procedures for this analysis.

Sheridan, Jean. "Teaching Part-Time MBAs to Use a Library." *Research Strategies* 3 (Fall 1985): 184-190.

Sheridan compares bibliographic instruction of adult students in behavioral sciences with those in business studies. Guidelines for a new BI model directed at MBA students are provided.

Stanger, Keith J. "How Responsive Is Bibliographic Instruction in the Needs of Users?" *Reference Services Review* 13 (Fall 1985): 55-58.

The author discusses bibliographic instruction in terms of satisfying user needs. Methods are suggested to reduce users' time to research information.

Strickland-Hodge, B. "Training Pre-Clinical Medical Students in the Use of the Library." *ISGN News* 30 (August 1985): 13-15.

Ternberg, Milton G. "BI for Accounting Students." *College and Research Libraries News* 46 (June 1985): 293-294.

Ternberg describes a joint library/business school project to experiment with the use of online business databases in an accounting course at the University of California, Berkeley.

Thaxton, Lyn. "Dissemination and Use of Information of Psychology Faculty and Graduate Students: Implications for Bibliographic Instruction." *Research Strategies* 3 (Summer 1985): 116-124.

Thaxton summarizes a study to assess the effectiveness of information dissemination in psychology. Graduate students as well as faculty were surveyed with the result that personalized bibliographic instruction and greater involvement of psychology faculty is needed.

Thesing, Jane I. "Marketing Academic Library Bibliographic Instruction Programs: Case and Commentary." *Research Strategies* 3 (Winter 1985): 29-36.

Thesing presents a case study of the rise and fall of a typical academic library instruction program as seen from the marketing point of view. Procedures are suggested to develop programs for a higher degree of user satisfaction.

Thompson, Glenn J. and B.R. Stevens. "Library Science Students Develop Pathfinders." *College and Research Libraries News* 46 (May 1985): 224-225.

The authors describe how the undergraduate reference course at the University of Wisconsin-Eau Claire helped to implement a reference pathfinder project to help students with research projects.

Turnage, Marthea. "User Education." *Texas Library Journal* 61 (Winter, 1985): 112-113,128-129.

Turnage discusses user instruction in terms of online catalogs and as compared to card catalogs. Various online catalog systems are compared.

VanPulis, Noelle. *User and Staff Education for the Online Catalog.* ERIC Reproduction Service, 1985. ED 257 478.

VanPulis describes methods used at Ohio State University to teach users and staff the use of the online catalog.

Vincent, C. Paul. "How about the *Readers' Guide?*" *Research Strategies* 3 (Spring 1985): 87-89.

The author suggests some not-so-well-known facts about the *Readers' Guide* and its part in bibliographic instruction.

Ward, Sandra N. "Course-Integrated DIALOG Instruction." *Research Strategies* 3 (Spring 1985): 52-64.

Ward describes hands-on DIALOG labs to teach students information retrieval strategies at Stanford University. Detailed procedures and strategies are included.

Wesley, Threasa L. and N. Campbell. "From Desk to Blackboard: A Practitioner's Approach to Teaching Reference." *The Southeastern Librarian* 35 (Winter 1985): 109-111.

The authors describe a reference course taught to graduate students in the University of Kentucky College of Library and Information Science by two practicing librarians. Included in the course were modules on reference collection development and bibliographic instruction.

Wiggins, Marvin E. and E. Wahlquist. "Independent Library Usage: A Research Strategy." *Journal of Academic Librarianship* 11 (November 1985): 293-296.

These authors describe a specific research unit in the freshman English composition course at Brigham Young University that teaches students independent research strategies for preparing papers.

Wilson, Lizabeth A. *The Connection between Library Skills Instruction and the Developmental Writer: Administrative Implications.* ERIC Reproduction Service, 1985. ED 256-372.

Wilson gives brief descriptions of three administrative options for implementing bibliographic instruction programs for college students. These involve composition instructors alone, librarians offering separate library skills courses, and cooperative programs by instructors and librarians.

York, Charlene C. "Tracing the Legislative Process." *Research Strategies* 3 (Spring 1985): 96-97.

York presents an assignment on tracing the legislative process of a federal law for a course-integrated library instruction module.

SCHOOL LIBRARIES

Aversa, Elizabeth. "Teaching Online Searching: A Review of Record Research and Some Recommendations for School Media Specialists." *School Library Media Quarterly* 13 (Summer 1985): 215-220.

Bell, I.W. and J.E. Wieckert. *Basic Media Skills Through Games.* 2 vols. 2d ed. Littleton, CO: Libraries Unlimited, 1985.

A wide variety of 112 games that teach library skills to elementary school students are presented including computer games. The authors provide grade levels, time, purpose, suitable number of students, materials, and procedures.

Berglund, Patricia. "School Library Technology." *Wilson Library Bulletin* 59 (January 1985): 336-337.

Berglund discusses an online catalog in the elementary school setting and how it helps children master library skills as well as how it motivates them to use the library.

Craver, Kathleen W. "Teaching Online Bibliographic Searching to High School Students." *Top Of the News* (Winter 1985): 131-138.

Craver describes a library instruction project for high school students that teaches them online searching and appropriate search strategies. All relevant documentation, a course outline, and a test are included.

Didier, Elaine K. "An Overview of Research on the Impact of School Library Media Programs on Student Achievement." *School Library Media Quarterly* 14 (Fall 1985): 33-36.

Faulkner, Ronnie W. *Help for the "Truly Needy": The Utilization Of Limited Resources by Secondary Teachers.* ERIC Reproduction Service, 1985. ED 261 702.

Faulkner presents a document for professional development of secondary teachers in the area of teaching library use.

Fiebert, Elyse E. "The Integration of Online Bibliographic Instruction into the High School Library Curriculum." *School Library Media Quarterly* 13 (Spring 1985): 96-99.

Fiebert describes Radnor (Pennsylvania) High School's extensive user instruction program including online searching for ninth graders. She also discusses the impact of having the library be a teaching center.

Gawith, Gwen. "Information Technology and Educational Librarianship." *New Zealand Libraries* 44 (March 1985): 157-159.

The author compares school use of technology in British libraries to use of technology in New Zealand school libraries. She also discusses impact on user education.

Gibbs, Sally E. "The Library as an Attitude of Mind: The Role of the Library in the Primary School." *The School Librarian* 33 (December 1985): 309-315.

Hackman, M.H. *Library Media Skills and the Senior High School English Program.* Littleton, CO: Libraries Unlimited, 1985.

Hackman discusses the cooperative role of English teachers and librarians to teach relevant library skills to senior high school students in a source-integrated mode. Practical advice, sample materials, and library skills programs from other states are provided.

Haines, Roberta M., et al. *Native American--Eskimo Media Skills Handbook.* ERIC Reproduction Service, 1985. ED 259 864.

The authors present library and media skills lessons for students in Kindergarten through ninth grades using information about native Americans and Eskimos.

Hales, Celia. "Basic BI at the University of North Carolina at Charlotte: Results of an Experiment." *The Southeastern Librarian* 35 (Fall 1985): 76-77.

Hales describes the library instruction program at the University of North Carolina at Charlotte and how evaluations have helped to change and improve it.

Hart, Thomas L. *Instruction in School Library Media Center Use (K-12).* 2d ed. Chicago: American Library Association, 1985.

This is an index to a multitude of instructional activities, games, tests, microcomputer soft-

ware, media material, and instructional strategies. It demonstrates that activities in library instruction have increased much since 1978. The book provides a section on testing, searching methods, and techniques, as well as reprints of many pertinent articles. Sections on reference tools, equipment operation, and a lengthy bibliography complete the work.

Haycock, Ken. "Teach-Librarians--Continuing to Build." *Canadian Library Journal* 42 (February 1985): 27-33.

Haycock discusses the role of teacher-librarian in the schools and how it can be strengthened and enhanced. He offers strategies for close cooperation within the curriculum to teach relevant research and study skills.

Hodges, Yvonne A., et al. "High School Students' Attitudes Towards the Library Media Program--What Makes the Difference?" *School Library Media Quarterly* 13 (Summer 1985): 183-190.

Joy, Hilda L. "Why Hasn't Anyone Told Me This Before?" *School Library Journal* 31 (March 1985): 124.

Joy discusses the need for teaching catalog filing rules and indexing skills to students as well as teachers. She offers methods for teaching such skills as well.

Kuhlthau, Carol C. "A Process Approach to Library Skills Instruction." *School Library Media Quarterly* (Winter 1985): 35-40.

The author investigates the library research process and how to teach it to high school students using a cognitive process. A timeline and details for teaching the research process are provided.

Lashbrook, John E. "Library Media Skills in the Classroom and the Library Media Center." *Ohio Media Spectrum* 37 (Spring 1985): 32-34.

Lashbrook summarizes an investigation to see how information is transformed into knowledge by fifth grade students and assesses the interaction of classroom instruction and library media skills.

Leisner, James W. "Learning at Risk: School Library Media Programs in an Information World." *School Library Media Quarterly* 14 (Fall 1985): 11-20.

Leisner advocates redesigning library skills programs in schools to incorporate the new technologies.

Leonard, P.B. *Choose, Use, Enjoy, Share; Library Media Skills for the Gifted Child.* Littleton, CO: Libraries Unlimited, 1985.

The author presents library media skills instruction methodology as an integral part of the elementary school curriculum based on experiences at Belmont Elementary School in Olney, Maryland.

Machalow, Robert. *Theodore Roethke: Microcomputer Bibliographic Instruction.* ERIC Reproduction Service, 1985. ED 262 776.

Machalow describes four steps needed to produce a software package for micros, which is designed to teach library skills to elementary school students. The topic of Theodore Roethke is used as an example information search.

Master, Lawrence S., et al. *A Librarian's Guide for Teaching a Nine-Week's Unit on Basic Reference and Bibliographic Skills to Academically Talented Junior High School Students.* ERIC Reproduction Service, 1985. ED 260 547.

The authors describe a nine-week course of reference and library skills for junior high school students taught by school librarians.

Muldoon, J.P. "Library Skills: A Lifelong Necessity." *NASSP Bulletin* 69 (April 1985): 98-99.

Muldoon offers suggestions for teaching library skills to high school students.

Perino, John A. "A Mastery of Media Skills Summer Program." *School Library Journal* 31 (May 1985): 50.

Perino describes a comprehensive reading and library skills program for students in grades five through nine.

Roberts, Beverly J. and I. Schon. "Student Aides in Arizona School Libraries: A Descriptive Study." *School Library Journal* 31 (May 1985): 32-35.

Roberts and Schon describe a study of elementary students used as library aides in Arizona. Details are given on how they are used and trained, and how they perform.

Schon, Isabel, et al. "The Effects of a Special Motivational Library Program on High School Students' Library Use and Attitudes." *Journal of Experimental Education* 54 (Fall 1985): 40-43.

The authors describe an experiment in five high schools that involved half of the students in a sophomore English class. The students were provided with an eight-week library instruction module to help improve their library skills and their library attitude.

Sline, Marjory. "Information Skills Teaching. A User Education Programme in a Post-Primary School." *School Librarian* 33 (June 1985): 115-120.

Sline gives an explanation of user education. She describes a user education program for middle school students in Great Britain including its evaluation.

Sneider-Brown, Jan. "Are You Happy with Your Library Skills Program?" *The Unabashed Librarian* 53 (1985): 9-10.

The author provides some guidelines for assessing library skills programs in a school setting and offers methods for the media specialist to become more integrated into the teaching process.

Svnicki, Marilla D. "Getting Down to the Basics of Teaching." *Catholic Library World* 56 (March 1985): 335-337, 344.

Svnicki offers strategies for successful teaching. She includes reactions from others in high school teaching situations.

Walisser, Sharon. "Developing a School-Based Research Strategy, K-7." *Emergency Librarian* 13 (September-October 1985): 19-26.

The author suggests strategies for teaching library research skills to students in grades kindergarten through seventh. Samples, outlines, and a glossary are provided.

Webb, C. Anne. "Modeling Recreational Reading: A Model." *English Journal* 74 (September 1985): 82-83.

Webb discusses the importance of browsing and of teaching library skills within the educational process.

SPECIAL LIBRARIES

Foreman, Gertrude E. and M.H. Mueller. "A Credit Course for Medical Students." *Medical Reference Service Quarterly* 4 (Fall 1985): 61-66.

The authors present information skills to health sciences students for professional use and continuing education in a two-credit course setting.

LaRue, J. and J.B. Holland. "Biblioprotocol: With a Brief Glossary of Terms Often Needed in Austrian and German Music Libraries." *Notes* 42 (September 1985): 29-35.

Martin, Jane F. and B.G. Dutton. "Online End-User Training: Experiences in a Large Industrial Organization." *Program* 19 (October 1985): 351-358.

Martin and Dutton describe the training of end-users in a company setting using an IBM PC and simulations. They also discuss implications for information scientists. Log-on procedures proved to be the most difficult task.

Sparks, Marie C. "A Dental Library Instruction Program." *Medical Reference Service Quarterly* 4 (Fall 1985): 427-436.

Sparks provides an outline for a library instruction program aimed at students in Indiana University's School of Dentistry. Objectives, methodology, and an evaluation are given.

Wanat, Camille. "Management Strategies for Personal Files: The Berkeley Seminar." *Special Libraries* 76 (Fall 1985): 253-260.

Wanat discusses an instructional program that advises and teaches researchers about access to and use of reprint collections.

ALL LEVELS

Brudin, Robert E. "Education for Instructional Librarians: Development and Overview." *Journal of Education for Library and Information Science* 25 (Winter 1985): 177-189.

Brudin discusses how library school curricula has been neglecting the training of librarians for bibliographic instruction. Some rationale for this neglect and a brief overview of the instructional program at the University of Alberta library school are provided.

Crowe, William J. "Library Skills for Students Keeping Pace." *OLA Bulletin* 55 (April 1985): 22-23.

Crowe provides a rationale for the establishment of an interorganizational task force on library instruction in Ohio.

Farley, Laine. "User Education." *Texas Library Journal* 61 (Summer 1985): 40-41, 64.

Farley discusses cooperative methods among different types of libraries that provide user instruction instigated by the academic library. He also advocates including local library information in academic library instruction programs.

Hamilton, Dennis. "Library Users and Online Systems: Suggested Objectives for Library Instruction." *RQ* 25 (Winter 1985): 195-197.

The author presents objectives for library instruction related to online systems, which can be used for instruction in all types of libraries.

Haynes, Evelyn. "Computer Assisted Library Instruction: An Annotated Bibliography." *Colorado Libraries* 11 (March 1985): 31-35.

This annotated bibliography includes references to items dealing directly with computer programs to teach library use.

Heinzhill, Richard. "Instructing Students in the Use of a Public OCLC Terminal." *PNLA Quarterly* 49 (Summer 1985): 14-16.

Heinzhill discusses a methodology to teach students the use of a public OCLC terminal as a reference tool.

Kohl, David F. *Reference Services and Library Instruction. A Handbook for Library Management.* Santa Barbara, CA: ABC-CLIO, 1985.

The second part of this handbook summarizes about twenty-five years of quantitative library research on library instruction from thirty-four key journals. A quick subject guide provides twenty-five access points and allows for scanning. It covers all types of libraries and includes an author index.

Kupersmith, John. "The Macintosh as a Sign Machine." *Research Strategies* 3 (Fall 1985): 178-180.

Kupersmith discusses the use of the Macintosh microcomputer for sign production and gives sample applications.

_____. "Not Just Another Wall: Library Suggestion Boxes." *Research Strategies* 3 (Spring 1985): 90-92.

The author advocates the use of suggestion boxes and bulletin boards to obtain user responses to the library sign system.

_____. "Signs of Change." *Research Strategies* 3 (Spring 1985): 37-39.

Kupersmith discusses the need for providing an effective sign system to accommodate a constantly changing environment. This system should be based on coordination, speedy production, and consistent and flexible displays.

Lubans, John, Jr. "Library Literacy." *RQ* 25 (Fall 1985): 47-50.

The author parallels user education developments to *RQ*'s history. His conclusions are that both have come a long way--user instruction needs more evaluation, and the librarian-teacher partnership needs more development.

_____. "Library Literacy." *RQ* 24 (Summer 1985): 381-383.

Lubans discusses librarians' reactions to the *Nation at Risk* report, and gives his recommendations for teaching library skills across the elementary and secondary curriculum.

Malley, Ian. *The Basics of Information Skills Teaching.* London: Clive Bingley, 1984.

Malley discusses information skills teaching in the broader sense, thus including study skills, communication skills, and reading and learning skills. The book addresses small library or information units in college, school, public, and special libraries and aims to be a practical guide to information skills programs.

Michaels, Carolyn. *Library Literacy Means Life-long Learning*. Metuchen, NJ: Scarecrow Press, 1985.

This monograph, written in a patchwork stream of consciousness format, discusses librarians' role in lifelong learning and related educational activities. It provides summaries and commentaries on theory, rationale, professional education, strategies, and measurement of library literacy as a means to lifelong learning.

Popp, Mary P. "Library Instruction Round Table: An Invitation and a Challenge." *Arkansas Librarian* 42 (June 1985): 5-6.

Popp discusses the importance of ALA's Library Instruction Round Table for any librarian interested in user instruction. LIRT's objectives, activities, and services are presented.

Rader, Hannelore B. "Library Orientation and Instruction--1984." *Reference Services Review* (Summer 1985): 61-78.

Rader provides an annual review of the library instruction literature in English, including short annotations for articles and books published in 1984.

Sugranes, Maria R. and L.C. Snider. "Microcomputer Applications for Library Instruction: Automation of Test and Assignment Scoring and Student Record Keeping." *Microcomputers for Information Management: An International Journal for Library and Information Services* 2 (September 1985): 171-188.

Sugranes and Snider describe an automated, library instruction records management system using microcomputers. Developmental stages of the system are provided.

Sullivan, Patricia and P. Seiden. "Educating Online Catalog Users." *Library Hi Tech* 10 (1985): 11-19.

The authors discuss methods of studying and evaluating the use of online public access catalogs and compare them to the protocol method. Major blocks to success were classified, and strategies to eliminate them were identified.

Other Bibliographies:

ACADEMIC END-USERS AND ONLINE SEARCHING: LIBRARY SERVICES AND INSTRUCTION 1984-1986
by the
ACRL/BIS Computer Concerns Committee

Crooks, James. "End User Searching at the University of Michigan Library." In *National Online Meeting Proceedings--1985*, compiled by Martha E. Williams and Thomas H. Hogan, 99-110. Medford, NJ: Learned Information, 1985.

Des Chene, Dorice. "Online Searching by End Users." *RQ* 25 (Fall 1985): 89-95.

Dodd, Jane, Charles Gilreath, and Geraldine Hutchins. *Texas A&M University Library. A Final Report from the Public Services Research Projects. A Comparison of Two End User Operated Search Systems. One of a Series of Self-Studies and Research Projects.* Bethesda, MD: ERIC Document Reproduc-tion Service, 1985. ED 255 224.

Friend, Linda. "Identifying and Informing the Potential End-User: Online Information Seminars." *Online* 10 (January 1986): 47-56.

_____. "Independence at the Terminal: Training Student End Users to Do Online Literature Searching." *Journal of Academic Librarianship* 11 (July 1985): 136-141.

Garman, Nancy J. and Judith M. Pask. "End User Searching in Business and Management." In *National Online Meeting Proceedings--1985*, compiled by Martha E. Williams and Thomas H. Hogan, 161-165. Medford, NJ: Learned Information, 1985.

Grotophorst, Clyde W. "Training University Faculty as End-Use Searchers: A CAI Approach." In *National Online Meeting Proceedings--1984*, compiled by Martha E. Williams and Thomas H. Hogan, 77-82. Medford, NJ: Learned Information, 1984.

Halperin, Michael and Ruth A. Pagell. "Free 'Do-It-Yourself' Online Searching...What to Expect." *Online* 9 (March 1985): 82-84.

Hunter, Janne A. "When Your Patrons Want to Search--The Library as Advisor to End Users...a Compendium of Advice and Tips." *Online* 8 (May 1984): 36-41.

Ifshin, Steven L. and Deborah M. Hull. "CAI Plus: A Strategy for COLLEAGUE Training." In *National Online Meeting Proceedings--1985*, compiled by Martha E. Williams and Thomas H. Hogan, 233-240. Medford, NJ: Learned Information, 1985.

Janke, Richard V. "Presearch Counseling for Client Searchers (End-Users)." *Online* 9 (September 1985): 13-26.

_____. "Online after Six: End User Searching Comes of Age." *Online* 8 (November 1984): 15-22.

Kirby, Martha and Naomi Miller. "Medline Searching on BRS COLLEAGUE: Search Success of Untrained End Users in a Medical School and Hospital." In *National Online Meeting Proceedings--1985*, compiled by Martha E. Williams and Thomas H. Hogan, 255-263. Medford, NJ: Learned Information, 1985.

Klausmeier, Jane A. "Microcomputer Based System for End User Training." In *National Online Meeting Proceedings--1985*, compiled by Martha E. Williams and Thomas H. Hogan, 265-271. Medford, NJ: Learned Information, 1985 (MICROsearch).

Kleiner, Jane P. "User Searching: A Public Access Approach to Search Helper." *RQ* 24 (Summer 1985): 442-451.

Lucia, Joseph and Christine Roydson. "Online Searching as an Educational Technology: Teaching Computer-Wise End Users." In *National Online Meeting Proceedings--1984*, compiled by Martha E. Williams and Thomas H. Hogan, 187-193. Medford, NJ: Learned Information, 1984.

Lyon, Sally. "End User Searching of Online Databases: A Selective Annotated Bibliography." *Library Hi Tech* 2 (1984): 47-50.

Mader, Sharon and Elizabeth H. Park. *Recommendation to Continue the BRS/After Dark End User Search Service.* Bethesda, MD: ERIC Document Reproduction Service, 1984. ED 252 215.

Mancall, Jacqueline C. "Training Students to Search Online: Rationale, Process, and Implications." *Drexel Library Quarterly* 20 (Winter 1984): 64-68. (High school students).

Penhale, Sara and Nancy Taylor. "Integrating End User Searching into a Bibliographic Instruction Program." *RQ* 25 (Spring 1986). Forthcoming.

Slingluff, Deborah, Yvonne Lev, and Andrew Eisan. "An End User Search Service in an Academic Health Sciences Library." *Medical Reference Services Quarterly* 4 (Spring 1985): 11-21.

Smith, Rita H. and Linda L. Phillips. "Search Helper: An Online Service for Undergraduates." *Reference Services Review* 12 (Fall 1984): 31-34.

Steffen, Susan Swords. "College Faculty Goes Online: Training Faculty to Search in a Liberal Arts In *Online '84 Conference Proceedings*, 232-238. Weston, CT: Online, 1984.

Trzebiatowski, Elaine. "End User Study on BRS/After Dark." *RQ* 23 (Summer 1984): 446-450.

Ward, Sandra and Laura M. Osegueda. "Teaching University Student End-Users about Online Searching." *Science and Technology Libraries* 5 (Fall 1984): 17-31.

Woolpy, Sara and Nancy Taylor. "Enduser Searching: A Study of Manual vs. Online Searching by Endusers and the Role of the Intermediary." In *Online '84 Conference Proceedings*, 243-245. Weston, CT: Online, 1984.

COMPUTERIZED INFORMATION RETRIEVAL: A LIBRARY SERVICE

Champlin, Peggy. "The Online Search: Some Perils and Pitfalls." *RQ* 25 (Winter 1985): 213-217.

Dreifuss, Richard A. "Library Instruction in the Database Searching Context." *RQ* 21 (Spring 1982): 233-238.

Gilreath, Charles. *Computer Literature Searching: Research Strategies and Databases.* CT: Westview Press, 1984.

Halperin, Michael. "Free Do-It-Yourself Online Searching...What to Expect." *Online* 9 (March 1985): 82-84.

Hamilton, Dennis. "Library Users and Online Systems: Suggested Objectives for Library Instruction." *RQ* 25 (Winter 1985): 195-197.

Knapp, Sara D. "Instructing Library Patrons about Online Reference Services." *The Bookmark* 38 (Fall 1979): 237-242.

_____. "Turf to Be Relinquished Cheerfully." *Journal of Academic Librarianship* 11 (November 1985): 272-273.

Kusack, James M. "Integration of Online Reference Service." *RQ* 19 (Fall 1979): 64-69.

Osegueda, Laura and Judy Reynolds. "Introducing Online Skills into the University Curriculum." *RQ* 22 (Fall 1982): 10-11.

Stewart, Linda Guyotte and James Markiewicz. "Teaching Information Retrieval: Lessons from Cornell." *Wilson Library Bulletin* 60 (March 1986): 32-34.

Tobin, Carol. "Online Computer Bibliographic Searching as an Instructional Tool." *Reference Services Review* 12 (Winter 1984): 71-73.

EDUCATING THE END-USER:
A LOEX 1986 BIBLIOGRAPHY

Avery, Elizabeth. "Teaching Online Searching: A Review of Recent Research and Some Recommendations for School Media Specialists." *School Library Media Quarterly* 13 (Summer 1985): 215-220.

Brooks, Kristina M. "Non-Mediated Usage of Online Retrieval Systems in an Academic Environment." In *Proceedings of the Third National Online Meeting, 1982*, 35-39. Medford, NJ: Learned Information,1982.

　　End-user instruction program at Oregon State University.

Champlin, Peggy. "The Online Search: Some Perils and Pitfalls." *RQ* 25 (Winter 1985): 213-217.

Dalrymple, Prudence W. "Closing the Gap: The Role of the Librarian in Online Searching." *RQ* 24 (Winter 1984): 177-185.

Des Chene, Dorice. "Online Searching by End Users." *RQ* 25 (Fall 1985): 89-95.

Griffith, Jeffrey C. "Why Can't I Do It? Emerging Training Concerns of End Users and Online Professionals." In *Online '83 Conference Proceedings*, 77-82. Medford, NJ: Learned Information, 1984.
　　Faculty end-user training program at George Mason University.

Haines, Judith S. "Experiences in Training End User Searchers." *Online* 6 (November 1982): 14-23.
　　Chemists as end-users searchers at Eastman Kodak.

Hamilton, Dennis. "Library Users and Online Systems: Suggested Objectives for Library Instruction." *RQ* 25 (Winter 1985): 195-197.
　　From the ALA RASD MARS Committee.

Hunter, Janne A. "When Your Patrons Want to Search- The Library as Advisor to End Users...a Compendium of Advice and Tips." *Online* 8 (May 1984): 36-41.

Kirk, Cheryl. "End-User Training at the Amoco Research Center." *Special Libraries* 77 (Winter 1986): 20-27.

Kleiner, Jane. "User Searching: A Public Access Approach to Search Helper." *RQ* 24 (Winter 1986): 442-451.

Marleski, Susan. "End-User Training: A Model for the Information Professional." In *Online '82 Conference Proceedings*, 25-30. Weston, CT: Online, 1982.
　　Elements of designing and implementing an end-user training program.

Smith, Rita H. and Linda L. Phillips. "Search Helper: An Outline Service for Undergraduates." *Reference Services Review* 12 (Fall 1984): 31-34.

Snow, Bonnie. "DIALOG Seminar for Medical Professionals." In *Proceedings of the Fifth National Online Meeting--1984*, 367-371. Medford, NJ: Learned Information, 1984.

Virgil, Peter J. "End-User Training: The Systems Approach." In *Proceedings of the Fifth National Online Meeting--1984*, 419-422. Medford, NJ: Learned Information, 1984.

Walton, Kenneth R. and Patricia Dedert. "Experiences at Exxon in Training End-Users to Search Technical Databases Online." *Online* 7 (September 1983): 42-50.

Ward, Sandra and L.M. Osegueda. "Teaching University Student End-Users about Online Searching." *Science & Technology Librarian* 5 (Fall 1984): 17-31.

INSTRUCTION IN ONLINE
SEARCHING IN SCHOOLS

Aversa, Elizabeth. "Teaching Online Searching: A Review of Recent Research and Some Recommendations for School Media Specialists." *School Library Media Quarterly* 13 (Summer 1985): 215-220.

Brophy, Edward. "Providing Online Search Services in High Schools." *Catholic Library World* 58 (1986): 35-39.

Craver, Kathleen W. "Teaching Online Bibliographic Searching to High School Students." *Top of the News* 41 (Winter 1985): 131-138. Also ERIC Document ED 244 633.

Fiebert, Elyse Evans. "The Integration of Online Bibliographic Instruction into the High School Curriculum." *School Library Media Quarterly* 13 (Spring 1985): 96-99.

Kachel, Debra E. "Online Bibliographic Searching: A Pilot Project." *Library Journal* 111 (May 1986): 28-30.

Mancall, Jacqueline C. and M. Carl Drott. "Materials Used by High School Students in Preparing Independent Study Projects: A Bibliometric Approach." *Library Research* 1 (Fall 1979): 223-236.

Schrader, Susan. *A Curriculum Guide for Online Database Searching with High School Students.* 1985. ERIC Document ED 256 373.

Tenopir, Carol. "Online Searching in Schools." *Library Journal* 108 (February 1986): 60-61.

Wozny, Lucy Anne. "Online Bibliographic Searching and Student Use of Information: An Innovative Teaching Approach." *School Library Media Quarterly* 10 (Fall 1982): 35-42.

Online Searching Guides:
Participants

FOURTEENTH NATIONAL LOEX LIBRARY INSTRUCTION CONFERENCE

Hoyt Center--Eastern Michigan University--8-9 May 1986

Bibliographic Instruction and Computer Database Searching Roster

Allegri, Francesca
Head of Information Management
Health Science Library
University of North Carolina
Chapel Hill, NC 27514

Arnold, Peggy
Reference Librarian
Baker College Library
1110 Eldon Baker Dr.
Flint, MI 48507

Arnott, Patricia
BI Coordinator
University of Delaware Library
Newark, DE 19717-5267

Baker, Betsy
BI Services Librarian
Northwestern University Library
Evanston, IL 60201

Balius, Sharon
Reference Librarian
Engineering Libraries
University of Michigan
Ann Arbor, MI 48109

Blowers, G. Elaine
Library Instruction Librarian
Libraries
Northern Illinois University
DeKalb, IL 60115

Bobay, Julie
Instruction Librarian
Libraries
Indiana University
Bloomington, IN 47405

Bradigan, Pamela S.
Head of Reference
Health Sciences Library
Ohio State University
Columbus, OH 43210

Brazer-Rush, Andrea
Librarian
Penfield Library
SUNY-Oswego
Oswego, NY 13126

Breitenwischer, Ann
Information Services
Ferris State College Library
Big Rapids, MI 49307

Brundage, Christina A.
Life Sciences Reference Librarian
Fenwick Library
George Mason University
4400 University Dr.
Fairfax, VA 22030

Bunge, Mary Beth
User Education Librarian
Main Library
Ohio State University
1858 Neil Avenue Mall
Columbus, OH 43210

Campbell, Douglas G.
Public Services Librarian
Libraries/Learning Resources
University of Wisconsin
Oshkosh, WI 54901

Campbell, John
Online Services Coordinator
University Libraries
University of Georgia
Athens, GA 30606

Carriar, Nancy
Social Sciences Reference Librarian
Library-Learning Resources Center
University of Minnesota-Duluth
Duluth, MN 55812

Cash, Michele
BI Coordinator/Head of Reference
Services
Library
Indiana University at South Bend
South Bend, IN 46635

Cassel, Jeris
Bibliographic Instruction Librarian
Folke Bernadotte Memorial Library
Gustavus Adolphus College
St. Peter, MN 56082

Cecora, Joan E.
ILL Coordinator/Reference Librarian
Hunt Library
Carnegie-Mellon University
Pittsburgh, PA 15213

Chambers, Saundra S.
Research Help Librarian
Shepard Memorial Library
North Carolina Central University
Durham, NC 27707

Chan, Betsy
Associate Librarian
Drake Memorial Library
SUNY College at Brockport
Brockport, NY 14420

Cheney, Debora
Database Searching Coordinator
Bertrand Library
Bucknell University
Lewisburg, PA 17837

Cichon, Joan
Assistant Professor
Library
Dayton Community College
Dayton, IL 60118

Codispoti, Margit
Sciences Reference Librarian
Helmke Library
Indiana University/Purdue University
  at Fort Wayne
Fort Wayne, IN 46805

Colman, Ronald P.
Access Services Librarian
Library
Eastern Michigan University
Ypsilanti, MI 48197

Cragg, Carole
Reference Librarian
Learning Resources Center
Bethel College
St. Paul, MN 55112

Crowley, Jean M.
Reference Librarian
Ireton Library
Marymount College of Virginia
Arlington, VA 22207

Davidge, Lyn
Associate Librarian
Graduate Library
University of Michigan
Ann Arbor, MI 48109

Davidson, Nancy M.
BI Coordinator/Reference Librarian
Dacus Library
Winthrop College
Rock Hill, SC 29733

Daye, Bennie E.
Business Reference Librarian
Shepard Memorial Library
North Carolina Central University
Durham, NC 27707

DeLong, Kathleen
Head- Information/Reference Services
Herbert T. Coutts Library
University of Alberta
Edmonton, Alberta Canada

DeMarinis, Ellen S.
BI Coordinator/Reference Librarian
Van Pelt Library
University of Pennsylvania
3420 Walnut St.
Philadelphia, PA 19104

Dimitroff, Alexandra
Reference Librarian
Welch Medical Library
Johns Hopkins University
Baltimore, MD 21205

Dowdey, Rosalie
Bibliographic Instruction Librarian
Mary Couts Burnett Library
Texas Christian University
Box 32904
Fort Worth, TX 76129

Engelbrecht, Pamela
General Reference Librarian
Newman Library
Virginia Tech
Blacksburg, VA 24061

Feldman, Beverly
Head of Reference
Silverman Undergraduate Library
SUNY at Buffalo
Buffalo, NY 14260

Frantz, Paul
Library Instruction Coordinator
Love Library
University of Nebraska-Lincoln
Lincoln, NB 68588-0410

Gillette, Meredith
Reference/Online Services Coordinator
Libraries and Learning Resources
University of Wisconsin
Oshkosh, WI 54901

Graybeal, Evelyn
Science & Technology Reference Librarian
Newman Library
Virginia Tech
Blacksburg, VA 24060

Groesbeck, Margaret Adams
Instruction/Online Bibliographic
  Retrieval Librarian
Library
Amherst College
Amherst, MA 01002

Hannon, Christine
Library Instruction Coordinator
Bracken Library
Ball State University
Muncie, IN 47306

Hansen, Edith L.
Reference/Instruction Librarian
Hutchins Library
Berea College
Berea, KY 40404

Harrison, Orion
Head Reference Librarian
Zach S. Henderson Library
Georgia Southern College
Statesboro, GA 30460-8074

Hart, Jim
Reference-Instruction Librarian
Central Library
University of Cincinnati
Cincinnati, OH 45221-0033

Horne, Dorice L.
Bibliographic Instruction Librarian
Library
Brooklyn College
Brooklyn, NY 11210

Howard, Pamela
Reference Librarian
Beeghly Library
Ohio Wesleyan University
Delaware, OH 43015

Iwami, Russell
Public Services Librarian
Sordoni-Burich Library
National College of Chiropractic
Lombard, IL 60148

Johnson, Shirley M.
Reference Librarian
Carlson Library
Clarion University of Pennsylvania
Clarion, PA 16412

Johnston, Patricia
Harriet Irving Library
University of New Brunswick
PO Box 7500
Fredericton, New Brunswick
Canada E3B 5H5

Jones, Deborah
Head- Reference Dept.
Irwin Library
Butler University
4600 Sunset Ave.
Indianapolis, IN 46208

Kelly, Bob
Science Reference Librarian
Library
University of Michigan-Dearborn
Dearborn, MI 48128

King, David
Graduate School of Library &
  Information Science
University of Illinois
Urbana, IL 61801

Kirkendall, Carolyn- Director
LOEX Clearinghouse
Eastern Michigan University
Ypsilanti, MI 48197

Kleiner, Jane P.
Head- Reference Services
Middleton Library
Louisiana State University
Baton Rouge, LA 70808

Kline, Nancy
Dept. Head- Library Instruction
Homer Babbidge Library
University of Connecticut
Stores, CT 06268

Kragness, Janice
Reference Librarian
Englebrecht Library
Wartburg College
Waverly, IA 50677

Kramer, Angela
Collections/Reference Librarian
Morisset Library
University of Ottawa
Ottawa, Ontario
Canada K1N 9A5

Lepkowski, Frank S.
Assistant Professor
Kresge Library
Oakland University
Rochester, MI 48063

Lincove, David A.
Online Searching Coordinator
Libraries
Ohio State University
Columbus, OH 43210

Lippincott, Joan A.
Head of Public Services
Mann Library
Cornell University
Ithaca, NY 14853-4301

Long, Julie
Reference/Instruction Librarian
Cushwa-Leighton Library
St. Mary's College
Notre Dame, IN 46556

Lowe, Myra N.
Reference Librarian
Library
West Virginia University
Morgantown, WV 26506

McGovern, Cass
Reference Librarian
College of Lake County
John C. Murphy Memorial Library
Grayslake, IL 60048

Mader, Sharon
Information Retrieval Librarian
Library
Memphis State University
Memphis, TN 38152

Markes, Paula
Reference Librarian/Database Coordinator
Libraries
Michigan State University
Lansing, MI

Mehok, Patricia
Bibliographic Instruction Librarian
Rockville Campus Library
Montgomery College
51 Mannakee St.
Rockville, MD 20850

Mensching, Glenn
Access Services Librarian
Library
Eastern Michigan University
Ypsilanti, MI 48197

Mensching, Teresa
LOEX Clearinghouse
Eastern Michigan University
Ypsilanti, MI 48197

Mertins, Barbara
Assistant Professor
Department of Library Science
West Virginia University
Morgantown, WV 26506-6069

Meyer, Wayne H.
Coordinator of Computer Search Service
Bracken Library
Ball State University
Muncie, IN 47306

Milne, Sally Jo
Reference/Instruction Librarian
Good Library
Goshen College
Goshen, IN 46526

Moore, Linda
Public Services Librarian
Mossey Center
Hillsdale College
Hillsdale, MI 49242

Musto, Fred
Reference Librarian
Main Library
Indiana University
Bloomington, IN 47405

Neveu, Ruth A.
Public Services Librarian
Shouldice Library
Lake Superior State College
Sault Ste. Marie, MI 49783

Nicholson, Donna
Microcomputer Services Coordinator
Library/Learning Center
University of Wisconsin-Parkside
Kenosha, WI 53141

Nixon, Henrietta J.
Reference and BI Librarian
Solomon R. Baker Library
Bentley College
Waltham, MA 02254

Okada, Emily
Reference/Instruction Librarian
Undergraduate Library
Indiana University
Bloomington, IN 47405

Owens, Gwen
Acting Head- Science Library
Marquette University
Milwaukee, WI 53233

Page, Richard
Library Instruction Librarian
Zimmerman Library
University of New Mexico
Albuquerque, NM 87131

Park, Betsy
Reference Librarian
Library
Memphis State University
Memphis, TN 38152

Penhale, Sara
Science Librarian
Wildman Science Library
Earlham College
Richmond, IN 47374

Perry, Martha S.
ILL/Reader Services Librarian
Library
Xavier University
Cincinnati, OH 45207

Piette, Mary
Reference Librarian
Merrill Library
Utah State University
Logan, UT 84322

Ramsdell, Kristin
Reference Librarian
Henry Memorial Library
Stanford University
Stanford, CA 94305

Robbins, Ronald E.
Head Reference Librarian
D.B. Skillman Library
Lafayette College
Easton, PA 18042

Rockman, Ilene
End-User Services Coordinator
Library
California Polytechnic State University
San Luis Obispo, CA 93406

Sabol, Laurie
Reference Librarian
Jerome Library
Bowling Green State University
Bowling Green, OH 43402

SantaVicca, Edmind F.
Humanities Reference Bibliographer
Libraries
Cleveland State University
Cleveland, OH 44114

Schichtel, Barbara Nan
Reference/Serials Librarian
Woodhouse LRC
Aquinas College
1607 Robinson Rd., SE
Grand Rapids, MI 49506

Schram, Wesley
Reference Librarian
Purdy/Kresge Libraries
Wayne State University
Detroit, MI 48073

Sette, Lynn
Reference Librarian
Yale Medical Library
New Haven, CT 06510

Shaw, Kay
BI/Reference Librarian
Milner Library
Illinois State University
Normal, IL 61761

Simmons-Welburn, Janice
Acting Head of the Medical Sciences
Library
Indiana University
Bloomington, IN 47405

Skekloff, Susan
Humanities Reference Librarian
Helmke Library
Indiana University-Purdue University
  at Fort Wayne
Fort Wayne, IN 46805

Snavely, Loanne
BI Coordinator/Reference Librarian
Bertrand Library
Bucknell University
Lewisburg, PA 17837

Snyder, Shirley A.
Head Librarian
Shenango Valley Campus Library
Pennsylvania State University
Sharon, PA 16146

Stanger, Keith
Coordinator of Access Services
Library
Eastern Michigan University
Ypsilanti, MI 48197

Stark, Marcella
Instructional Services Coordinator
Bird Library
Syracuse University
Syracuse, NY 13244-2010

Starr, Glen Ellen
Library Instruction Coordinator
Belk Library
Appalachian State University
Boone, NC 28608

Stebelman, Scott
BI/Reference Librarian
Gelman Library
George Washington University
Washington, DC 20052

Steffen, Susan Swords
Head
Schaffner Library
Northwestern University
339 E. Chicago Ave.
Chicago, IL 60611

Taylor, Nancy
Reference Librarian
Lilly Library
Earlham College
Richmond, IN 47374

Thompson, Dorothea M.
BI Coordinator/Reference Librarian
Hunt Library
Carnegie-Mellon University
Pittsburgh, PA 15213

Trupiano, Rose
Reference/Instruction Librarian
Library/Learning Center
University of Wisconsin-Parkside
Kenosha, WI 53141

Vastine, Jim
Coordinator of Bibliographic Instruction
Library
University of South Florida
Tampa, FL 33620

Voelck, Julie
Reference/Periodicals Librarian
Saginaw Valley State College Library
2250 Pierce Rd.
University Center, MI 48710-0001

Vyhnanek, Louis
Reference Librarian
Holland Library
Washington State University
Pullman, WA 99165

Walsh, Mary Jane
BI/Reference Librarian
Case Library
Colgate University
Hamilton, NY 13346

Ward, James E.
Director
Crisman Memorial Library
David Lipscomb College
Nashville, TN 37203

White-Carter, Anita
Reference Librarian
Ramsey Library
University of North Carolina
 at Asheville
Asheville, NC 28804

Williams, Pamela S.
BI Librarian
Library
Frostburg State College
Frostburg, MD 21532

Wilson, Barbara
Education Librarian
Houston Academy of Medicine-
 Texas Medical Center Library
Houston, TX 77036

Wright, Marie T.
Bibliographic Instruction Librarian
University Library
Indiana University-Purdue University
 at Indianapolis
Indianapolis, IN 46202

Wygant, Alice C.
Education Coordinator-Reference Librarian
Moody Medical Library
University of Texas Medical Branch
Galveston, TX 77550-2782

York, Charlene C.
Coordinator of Computer Searching
Jerome Library
Bowling Green State University
Bowling Green, OH 43403

Young, Victoria
Head of Reader Services
Xavier University Library
Cincinnati, OH 45207